UPDATE SERVICE
■ Introductory Offer ■

Our books are as current as we can make them, but sometimes the laws do change between editions. You can read about law changes which may affect this book in the NOLO NEWS, a 16-page newspaper which we publish quarterly.

In addition to the Update Service, each issue contains comprehensive articles, about the growing self-help law movement as well as areas of the law that are sure to affect you. **(regular subscription rate is $7.00)**

To receive the next 4 issues of the NOLO NEWS, please send us $2.00.

Name _____

Address _____

_____

Send to: NOLO PRESS, 950 Parker St., Berkeley, CA 94710

Recycle Your Out-of-Date Books & Get One Third off your next purchase!

Using an old edition can be dangerous if information in it is wrong. Unfortunately, laws and legal procedure change often. To help you keep up to date we extend this offer. If you cut out and deliver to us the title portion of the cover of any old Nolo book we'll give you a 33% discount off the retail price of any new Nolo book. For example, if you have a copy of TENANTS' RIGHTS, 4th edition and want to trade it for the latest CALIFORNIA MARRIAGE AND DIVORCE LAW, send us the TENANTS' RIGHTS cover and a check for the current price of MARRIAGE & DIVORCE, less a 33% discount. Information on current prices and editions are listed in the Nolo News (see above box). Generally speaking, any book more than two years old is of questionable value. Books more than four or five years old are a menace.

OUT OF DATE = DANGEROUS

This offer is to individuals only.

California Tenants' Handbook

Tenants' Rights

by California attorneys

Myron Moskovitz
Ralph Warner
Charles E. Sherman

Edited by Toni Lynne Ihara
Illustrations by Linda Allison

NOLO PRESS ■ 950 Parker St., Berkeley, CA 94710

PRINTING HISTORY

Nolo Press is committed to keeping its books up-to-date. Each new printing, whether or not it is called a new edition, has been completely revised to reflect the latest law changes.

First Edition	
First printing	August 1972
Second printing	January 1973
Second Edition	
First printing	May 1974
Second printing (revised)	February 1975
Third Edition	
First printing	November 1975
Second printing	April 1976
Fourth Edition	
First printing	January 1977
Second printing (revised)	December 1977
Third printing (revised)	August 1978
Fourth printing	July 1979
Fifth Edition	
First printing	January 1980
Sixth Edition	
First printing	March 1981
Seventh Edition	
First printing	August 1982
Second printing (revised)	February 1983
Eighth Edition	
First printing	February 1984
Second printing	July 1984
Third printing	January 1985

We wish to thank the following people associated with the first Moskovitz manuscript: Pedro Echeverria and Ronald Vera for their research assistance, Mary Durant and Madeline Finlay for their secretarial assistance, Allan David Heskin for his editorial assistance and Ann Curtis for her artwork.

We also wish to express our gratitude to some friends who helped to make this a better book. Thanks to Lucretia Edwards, Jeffrey Carter, Alan Verson, Paul Rosenthal, Carmen Massey and David Brown.

ISBN 0-917316-81-9

© Copyright 1972, 1981, 1982, 1984, 1985
by Myron Moskovitz, Ralph Warner and Charles Sherman

TABLE OF CONTENTS

INTRODUCTION   **10**

CHAPTER 1. SOME GENERAL THINGS YOU SHOULD KNOW   **13**
A. Who Is Your Landlord?   **13**
B. The Landlord Business   **15**
C. Lawyers   **18**
       1. What Lawyers Can Do For You   **19**
       2. When Do You Need A Lawyer?   **21**
       3. Finding A Lawyer   **21**
D. Renters' Tax Credit   **24**

CHAPTER 2. LOOKING FOR A PLACE, RENTING IT, MOVING IN   **25**
A. Get Organized   **25**
       1. Home and Apartment Locator Services   **26**
B. Learn About Rental Agreements   **26**
       The Three Kinds of Rental Agreements   **27**
       1. Oral Agreements   **27**
       2. Leases and Written Rental Agreements   **28**
       3. Common Provisions in Printed Forms and What to Watch Out For   **30**
       4. Which is Better, A Lease or Rental Agreement?   **33**
       5. Model Lease and Model Rental Agreement   **34**
C. Security Deposits, Cleaning Fees and Last Month's Rent   **35**
D. How to Check a Place Over Before You Rent It   **41**

E. How to Bargain for the Best Deal   46
F. Get All Promises in Writing   48
G. Self Protection When Moving In   51
H. Your Responsibilities as a Tenant   52
I. Co-Signing Leases   53

CHAPTER 3. SHARING A HOME   55
A. Is It Legal To Live Together?   55
B. The Legal Obligations of Roommates to the
    Landlord   56
C. Legal Obligations of Roommates to Each Other   58
D. Having A Friend Move In   60

CHAPTER 4. ALL ABOUT RENT   69

CHAPTER 5. DISCRIMINATION   73

**CHAPTER 6. THE OBNOXIOUS LANDLORD AND YOUR
            RIGHT TO PRIVACY**   79

**CHAPTER 7. SUBSTANDARD HOUSING CONDITIONS
            HOW TO GET REPAIRS MADE**   85
A. Your Rights—The Landlord's Duty   85
B. Getting Repairs Made   86
    1. Rent Withholding   89
    2. Go to the Local Authorities   94
    3. Repair It Yourself   96
    4. Sue the Landlord   99
    5. Move Out   100

**CHAPTER 8. INJURIES TO A TENANT DUE TO SUBSTANDARD
            HOUSING CONDITIONS**   103

**CHAPTER 9. BREAKING A LEASE AND OTHER LEASE
            PROBLEMS**   107
A. What Happens When the Lease Runs Out   107
B. How To Sublease   108
C. How To Break A Lease   110

**CHAPTER 10. MOVING OUT AND GETTING YOUR DEPOSITS
             BACK**   117
A. Giving Notice   117

   B. Getting Your Deposits Back (Rent Withholding,
      How To Use Small Claims Court)   118

CHAPTER 11. EVICTIONS   129
   A. Illegal Landlord Conduct   129
      1. Utility Cut-Off   129
      2. Lock-Out   130
   B. Summary of Eviction Procedure   131
   C. Planning What To Do   133
   D. Representing Yourself   134
      1. Negotiating A Settlement   135
      2. Technical Information   136
         a. Notice Requirements   136
         b. The Law Suit   139
         c. Outline Of An Eviction Law Suit   142
      3. Defending Yourself   144
   E. After The Eviction   153

CHAPTER 12. TENANTS ACTING TOGETHER   155
   A. Tenant Organizing   156
   B. Setting Up A Tenant's Union   160
   C. Getting Information On The Landlord   164
   D. Tactics   167
   E. Negotiations   173
   F. The Collective Bargaining Agreement   175

CHAPTER 13. RENTERS INSURANCE   185

CHAPTER 14. CONDOMINIUM CONVERSION   187

CHAPTER 15. RENT CONTROL   191

**APPENDIX 1. SAMPLE MODEL LEASE, MODEL RENTAL
            AGREEMENT AND CHECKLIST**   203

APPENDIX 2. THE FORM ANSWER-UNLAWFUL DETAINER   209

**APPENDIX 3. FORM INTERROGATORIES-UNLAWFUL
            DETAINER**   219

INTRODUCTION

For good or ill, the passage of Proposition 13 is an event that shapes our lives in the 1980s. Voters made a decision that had a direct, tangible effect on the lives of all who owned real property with the result that the property tax was dramatically lowered. But despite all the noble words of the Proposition 13 campaign in which landlords promised to share their tax savings with their tenants, the truth is that the large majority of landlords pocketed their property tax savings with one hand and raised rents with the other. Renters, however, quickly learned the larger lesson of the Proposition 13 campaign —that the political process is open to all who will organize to help themselves. Local tenant organizations blossomed across California like poppies in the spring and suddenly rent regulation ordinances were on the ballot almost everywhere. And even more exciting, tenants finally began to sense their political power and realize that in many communities they were the majority.

There are many possible legislative reforms in addition to rent control that might improve the condition of being a tenant in California. We will highlight a number of these in the text, but we also wish to refer you to an excellent statewide organization that is working daily to improve the lot of tenants. This is CHAIN, the California Housing Action and Information Network. CHAIN's non-profit educational arm, California Housing Research Foundation, publishes "CHAIN LETTER" quarterly, to keep tenants advised of the latest activity to protect their rights. The address of both is P.O. Box 20226, Oakland, California 94620.

But as much as we support action to improve the condition of being a tenant, this book is not essentially about law reform. Here our job is to inform you, the California tenant, of your legal and practical rights as they now exist. We aim here to simplify, to speak plainly to those who do not have legal training. As an informed tenant, there is much you can do to intelligently handle those problems that can't be avoided.

As you almost certainly understand already, California law is favorable to landlords as now written. The deck is stacked against the tenant even though there have been significant improvements in tenants' rights in the last few years. In most situations, you will find that the legislature has given your landlord a lot of protection while giving you very little. We can't magically re-stack the deck in this small book. We can, and do, give you a lot of information that will even the odds a little.

There are some who feel that this book is overly biased in favor of tenants and that the existence of bad tenants and good landlords is overlooked. To this charge we plead guilty. In these pages the landlord tends rather regularly to seem like an ogre. This does not mean that we preach that "badness" is necessarily in the nature of landlords, but, since this book is about problems seen from the tenant's point of view, we do focus upon all the foul deeds that landlords have been known to do. Yes, this book is purposely oriented around tenant's problems. Landlords have associations, lobbyists, lawyers and legislators to protect their interests, while tenants have few resources. This book is designed to change this imbalance. In short—this is a battle book.

It has to be said somewhere where it will stand out, so why not here: The heart of the tenant's problem is not the laws and regulations (imperfect though they may be), nor the goodness or badness of landlords (for they, like you, are but human)—no, the heart of the problem is with the supply of housing. It is drastically short. No matter how well you represent yourself, no matter how much the rules become improved, no matter how together tenants become, the basic rules of supply and demand will still allow landlords to rule the roost. Huge sums of public money are being spent daily, hourly, to feed the big machines that suck us all dry; but very little of that money ever sees its way into the life of the average person, and we fall pathetically short of all of our potentials for domestic harmony. If there were enough good places to go around, then many of the problems that this book is about would disappear as if by magic. That being said, we must move on, for nothing we can say here will immediately increase the housing supply, and there are some immediate tasks to be accomplished in the rest of these pages.

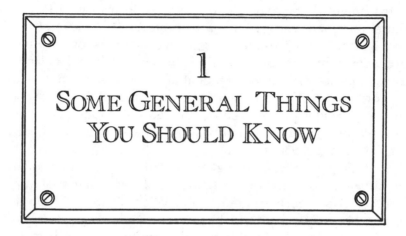

1
SOME GENERAL THINGS YOU SHOULD KNOW

A. WHO IS YOUR LANDLORD?

Know Your Landlord.* Your landlord may be a little old man with a Siamese cat and a bad head for arithmetic or you may rent from a large corporation. There is no typical landlord. In this book we give you a lot of information about your legal rights, but we can't tell you what kind of a landlord you have. It is extremely important that you find out what kind of person your landlord is, because having complete knowledge of your legal rights will help you very little if you lack a good human understanding of the person with whom you are dealing. Coupled with such an understanding this book can be of great value.

Along with understanding the personality of your landlord, it is important to know his or her problems, circumstances and style of operating. Dealing with a retired lady managing her late uncle's duplex will obviously be a lot different from dealing with an institution with 500 units, managers, rules and red tape.

---

*Of course, it is equally fair to say to a landlord "know your tenant and your legal rights." There is an excellent book available for landlords entitled *Landlording*. See the back of this book for a description.

Know Your Manager. Many medium to large apartment complexes have managers. The landlord wants to make money, but he wants somebody else to do the dirty work of actually managing the rental property. More and more landlords are hiring management corporations who specialize in managing lots of rental units and who get paid a percentage (about 10%) of the rental income. Such companies tend to be sticklers for rules and procedures, but are usually less emotionally involved than landlords, and are often more rational at arriving at business-like compromises.* Often, however, the landlord will simply give a student or older person free or reduced rent to look after his property on a part-time basis. Just as there are all sorts of landlords there is an equal variety of managers.

In dealing with your manager on a day to day basis, it is important not only to notice who he is and how best to deal with him; it is also important to notice his relationship to the landlord. Remember, the landlord and the manager may have very different interests. The landlord wants the property to yield a maximum amount of profits with a minimal amount of trouble, but the manager's major concern is probably doing as little work as possible for his free rent. In this sort of situation you may be able to deal directly with the landlord with good results. This is especially true if the premises are not being kept clean or in good repair or if the manager is impolite. In any case, where communications are sticky or broken down, you should consider sending duplicate copies of letters and other communications to the landlord as well as to the manager.

Finding Out the Name of Your Landlord. In the past, some landlords have instructed their managers not to tell the tenants who they were or where they could be located, so the tenant could not "bother" them. A new law which applies only to buildings with more than two dwelling units tries to solve this problem. California Civil Code §1962 now provides that:

---

*Usually a rental management corporation manages a lot of units in a relatively small geographic area. This makes checking their reputation fairly easy. It is wise to do so.

If the building or development has 16 or more apartments, there must be a resident manager living there. 25 California Administrative Code §66.

1. The rental agreement must state the name and address of both the manager and owner (or person authorized by him to receive notices, demands and law suits against the owner). This information must be kept current with the tenant being informed of all changes,

OR,

2. Instead of putting this information in each rental agreement the landlord may choose to post notices containing the same information in the building. A notice must be posted in two easy to see places including elevators if they exist.

If the landlord fails to follow this law, then the person who rented the dwelling for the landlord automatically becomes his agent for receiving notices, demands and law suits.

B. THE LANDLORD BUSINESS

You may choose not to read this section and still learn all you need to know about what you face as a tenant. For those who are interested, however, we thought it would be helpful to understand how the landlord business works. We believe that a tenant or group of tenants will be in a better position to make wise decisions if they have an idea of what it's like to walk a mile in their landlord's boots.

Making money as a landlord depends a great deal on making wise initial investment decisions and on having an ability to manage property. This is true whether the landlord owns one unit or a thousand units. Given average ability in these directions, however, it is pretty difficult to lose money in the landlord business. Indeed, many landlords achieve spectacular returns. This is possible because the landlord is able to take advantage of a number of favorable tax laws and is able to use **your money** to do it.

The landlord business works something like this. To buy a building or building complex the landlord must usually put down between 10% and 25% of the purchase price. A bank or insurance company puts up the rest. If he buys a decent building he is then able to set the rents at a level that will allow him to cover all of his mortgage, tax and upkeep payments and pocket a little money besides. If you ask a landlord about his yearly profit he will doubtless tell you that it is small, but will not tell you that each year he owns more of the building and in addition is receiving large tax deductions on his personal tax returns.

You have probably heard about "tax shelters" and "tax loopholes." There are many of these available to landlords. Here is how tax laws work to benefit landlords:

- All the money a landlord pays for building maintenance and upkeep expense is subtracted from the landlord's profit figure before taxes are paid;
- All the money that a landlord pays in the form of interest on his mortgage payments constitutes a tax deduction. In the early years of a mortgage, interest will run as high as 80% to 90% of each payment;
- All the money a landlord pays in local property taxes constitutes a tax deduction;
- A percentage of the value of a landlord's buildings is deductible each year under the heading of "depreciation." The depreciation deduction allows the landlord credit for wear and tear to his building and the fact that the building is supposed to get less valuable as it gets older. If a landlord claims that a particular building has a useful life of 20 years, he is able to deduct 5% of the building's value each year. In some situations, a landlord is able to take advantage of laws that allow him to take extra depreciation in the early years of a mortgage. The depreciation deduction is often a major windfall for a landlord. This is because in most cases a building is more valuable after 20 years than it was when first purchased. Thus, the landlord gets his yearly tax deduction and a more valuable building too. As soon as the depreciation credits are used up, the wisdom of the landlord business dictates that the building be sold to a new landlord who then declares a new life expectancy for the building and starts the depreciation process all over again.

So far we have seen that a landlord has bought a building with a little bit of his own money and a lot of borrowed money. He then collects rent from you and other tenants, then uses your rent money to pay off his loan (mostly interest in the first years) and to pay property taxes and upkeep. With the exception of the small amount of money that represents the principal portion of each mortgage payment, he can deduct everything else from his taxes. Of course, the richer he is to start with, the more valuable the tax deductions become. Is it any wonder that the rich can't afford not to buy property?

There are still more reasons why the landlord business is so profitable. Unlike income that you pay taxes on at ordinary rates, your landlord is able to treat any profit he makes from selling rental property as "capital gains." This means that he is taxed at a rate that is roughly half (and often less) of what he would normally pay. This can be enormously significant when apartment complexes are being bought and sold for millions of dollars. Landlords also get certain built-in advantages in times of inflation such as we are in now. A landlord benefits in that he is able to raise rental incomes while his mortgage and interest payments remain constant. In a similar way, the landlord often gets a break on his real property taxes. Normally, a building is assessed for local property tax purposes on the basis of the original purchase price. In periods of inflation, however, rental income often goes up faster than do tax assessments.

With so much in the landlord's favor, it is truly amazing that any landlords are in unfavorable financial situations. When such is the case, however, it always goes hard on the tenants. If the landlord is foolish or greedy, he may get over-extended on his loans (that is, he may try to buy too much property without enough money, or may have paid too much for the property in the first place). Then he will have to raise rents and/or cut back on repairs and services. This can lead to a high turn-over of dissatisfied or resentful tenants. Such circumstances can make the landlord harder to deal with, almost desperate.

NOTE: You may want to ask your landlord about his finances and problems, especially if you are on good terms. He might appreciate your interest (making for an easier relationship), and you may learn some things that will increase your understanding of his or her problems.

Landlords can be hurt quickly: (a) by periods of deflation and depression (the 1930's was a bad time for landlords) when they can't fill up their buildings with tenants at favorable rents; (b) by any action by tenants to jointly withhold rents, and (c) by extremely tough rent control ordinances. None of these conditions has been widespread in California in recent years. As a result landlords have done very well and in many cases have made enormous profits. To see that these profits keep coming, landlords have organized at the local, state and federal levels. Through real estate associations, apartment house owners associations and similar groups, landlords keep a close watch on everything from your local city council and planning commission to the state and federal legislatures. Lobbyists maintain offices in Sacramento and Washington with the specific purpose of furthering the landlord business and seeing to it that no law harmful to landlords is passed by any legislature anywhere. Landlord lobbyists are also very successful at getting legislation introduced and enacted that is favorable to landlords.

C. LAWYERS

This book is not designed to replace an attorney. It is meant to help you decide whether or not you **need** one. The law says that you have a right to have an attorney represent you if you want one; no law says that you must have one.

The lawyer is an expert with words. His special talent is knowing what to say, who to say it to, and when to say it. If you always knew what to say, who to say it to, and when to say it, you wouldn't need a lawyer! The lawyer has special knowledge and special experience to help you make decisions. If you have sufficient information and knowledge available to you to make your own decisions, there may be no need for a lawyer.

Lawyers are in business to make money. They have to pay a lot of office overhead as well as support themselves and their families in a style to which they are, or would like to be, accustomed. Thus, most charge fairly high fees, normally in a range of $50 to $100 an hour. Clearly, when you have a dispute with your landlord which involves a few hundred dollars, it does not make good sense to pay someone as much, or more, to try to vindicate your position. In addition, there is always the danger that you will lose and end up paying both your landlord and your attorney, too.

This book is designed to give you a clear understanding of your rights and obligations. Hopefully by gaining such an understanding before getting into a dispute, the dispute can be avoided.

This will not always be so, however, and disputes will occur in which some kind of legal service will be necessary.

1. WHAT LAWYERS CAN DO FOR YOU*

There are three basic ways a lawyer can help with the kinds of problems that face a tenant:

---

*Many people wish to do some of their own legal research before visiting a lawyer. County law libraries (which are located in main county courthouses) are free and open to the public. Unfortunately, legal materials are indexed in ways quite different from the systems in use in non-law libraries, and it can often be difficult to locate what you need. To decipher this foreign language, see **Legal Research: How to Find and Understand the Law** by Stephen Elias (order information at the back of this book).

a. Consultation and Advice

The lawyer can listen to the details of your situation, analyze it for you, and advise you on your position and best plan of action. Ideally he will give you more than just conclusions—he can educate you about your whole situation and tell you all the various alternatives available, then you can make your own choices. This kind of service is the least expensive as it only involves an office call and a little time. A charge of more than $30 to $50 for a consultation might be considered excessive. Find out the fee before you go in.

b. Negotiation

The lawyer can use his special talents, knowledge and experience to help you negotiate with the landlord to your best advantage. In case of serious problems, he can do this more successfully than you, especially if you are at odds with the landlord, or if your landlord has an attorney. Without spending much of his own time, he can often accomplish a lot through a letter or phone call. Receiving a message on an attorney's letterhead is, in itself, often very sobering to a landlord. He knows you mean business! A lawyer can sometimes possess considerable skill as a negotiator. Also, if bad turns to worse, a lawyer can often bluff by threatening legal action. You can then decide at a later time whether to actually pursue it.

c. Law Suits

In some instances your case may merit going into court with a law suit. Having your lawyer go into court is very expensive, and only rarely warranted. If the landlord sues you first, it is more likely that you will end up in court, and very likely that you will need a lawyer's help.

Whenever you think of using a lawyer, keep in mind this view of clients that is held by a lawyer-friend of ours: he imagines a man who has built a shack on some old railroad tracks in a high mountain valley. One day, when he puts his ear to the track, the man hears a distant vibration. A few days later he can hear the sound of a train rumbling on the warm breeze that blows up the canyon, and soon the sound is distinctly audible. At this point he can begin to see the smoke of the engine, and not much later the train is running down on him, spitting fire and belching smoke. When the thing is fifty yards away, he picks up his phone, calls his lawyer and asks him to get an injunction against the railroad company! What we mean to say is ... if you decide to use a lawyer, don't wait until it's too late.

2. WHEN DO YOU NEED A LAWYER?

There is no simple answer to the question of when you need a lawyer. This is because there are many possible areas of dispute between landlord and tenant, and many levels of tenant ability to deal with problems. Throughout this book we will suggest times when the advice or other services of an attorney would be useful, but here are a few general pointers:

a. If you have a lease or a written rental agreement which allows attorney fees for your landlord, then California law says that the tenant is also entitled to recover attorney fees if he wins a law suit based on the terms of that agreement;

b. If your landlord sues you for a lot of money, see an attorney;

c. If you have any problem that you can't understand or solve by reading this book, you should try to get some professional advice.

3. FINDING A LAWYER

Finding a lawyer who charges reasonable prices and whom you feel can be trusted is not always an easy task. There is always the fear that by just picking a name out of the telephone book you may get someone unsympathetic (perhaps an attorney who specializes in representing landlords) or an attorney who will charge too much. You should realize that these are common fears and that you are not the only one who feels a little scared and intimidated. Here are some suggestions:

a. Legal Aid

If you are **very** poor, you may qualify for free help from your Legal Aid office. Check your phone directory for their location, or ask your County Clerk.

b. Group Legal Practices

A new but rapidly growing aspect of California law practice is the Group Legal Practice program. Many groups, including unions, employers and consumer action groups, are offering plans to their members whereby they can get legal assistance for rates which are substantially lower than offered by most private practitioners. Some of these plans are good, some mediocre, and a few are not worth it, but most are better than nothing. You should watch out for plans that are little more than fronts for private law firms and which offer little in decision making. Because the group practices area of the law is changing so rapidly, we can't give you a statewide list of group legal plans.

c. Private Attorneys

If you don't know an attorney that can be trusted and can't get a reliable recommendation from a friend, you have a problem. While you might be lucky and randomly pick an attorney who matches your needs perfectly, you might just as easily wind up paying too much for too little. Here are some suggestions that should make your search a little easier:

- Check with a local tenant organization to see if they can recommend someone. This is probably the most effective way to find a lawyer in your area who is truly an advocate for the rights of tenants.
- Lawyers can now legally advertise. Check the yellow pages and other media for people who say they specialize in tenant problems. Organizations calling themselves "Legal Clinics" often provide help to tenants at a more reasonable price than do regular law firms. But don't assume that, because someone gives you a good pitch on T.V., they will really deliver what

they promise. Remember, someone has to pay for all that T.V. time.

- Referral panels set up by local bar associations. You can often find their number in the classified section of the newspaper under Attorneys. Lawyers are given some minimal screening as to their expertise in landlord-tenant law before qualifying to be listed. There is usually a small fee for an initial consultation. Many times you may get a good referral from these panels, but be sure to question the lawyer whose name you are given carefully about their qualifications as inexperienced lawyers do occasionally get listed. Also you will want to be sure that the person you are referred to is truly sympathetic to the rights of tenants.
- Shop around by calling different law offices and stating your problem. Ask them how much it would cost for a visit. Try to talk to a lawyer personally to attempt to get an idea of how friendly and sympathetic he or she is to your concerns.
- Remember, lawyers whose offices and life styles are reasonably simple are more likely to help you for less money than lawyers who feel naked unless wearing a $500 outfit. You should be able to find an attorney willing to discuss your problems for $30 to $50.

D. RENTERS' TAX CREDIT— CALIFORNIA INCOME TAX

California allows a tax credit of $60 for single people and $137 for married couples and heads of household to people who rent their principal dwelling place and who are not claimed as a dependent by another taxpayer.* If you pay taxes, you subtract the credit from the amount owed. If you don't pay taxes, you can still get the credit. This means you file a return and the state pays you. Married couples can only get one credit, but people living together can each claim one. In addition, tenants 62 years of age or older and whose annual income is $12,000 or less are eligible for tax benefits due to the fact that part of their rent is used to pay property taxes.** For technical details on these benefits, see the Individual Income Tax guide put out by the California Franchise Tax Board.

---

*Revenue and Taxation Code section 17053.5
**Revenue and Taxation Code section 19523.5

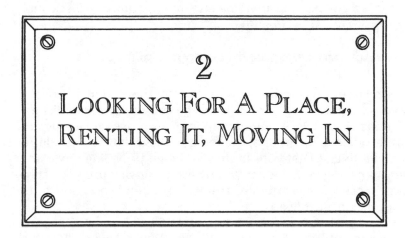

2
LOOKING FOR A PLACE, RENTING IT, MOVING IN

A. GET ORGANIZED

Looking for a house or apartment to rent is often a frustrating and time-consuming task. Since it is human nature to get harried and frazzled under pressure, many mistakes are made at this stage which later turn out to be costly, both in time and money. Try to stay cool.

Before you start looking for a place, decide how much you want to pay, how long you plan on staying and what sort of area you want to live in. Be realistic both as to your budget and as to what is available, and set definite guidelines in advance. If you find a place that fits your needs right away you should celebrate. But if you can't find a place that meets your guidelines, under no circumstances change them without taking time to think the matter over carefully. Some of the worst and most costly mistakes are made by people who sign a lease or put down a deposit at the end of a long frustrating day only to realize later that the place is completely unsuitable.

It is extremely important that you keep all records. As a part of your getting organized, get a large manilla envelope or file folder in which to keep all papers having to do with your rental transaction. Misplacing and losing papers (deposit agreements, leases, rent receipts, etc.) is a common mistake that should be avoided. Your landlord is in business and has probably learned how not to make such basic mistakes, so you should do the same. Set up a safe place in which to save your papers, receipts, cancelled checks, and anything else that you think might possibly be important at a later time.

1. HOME AND APARTMENT LOCATOR SERVICES

A number of companies advertise "home finding" services. Most of these charge an advance fee and then provide listings of available rentals. A number of these businesses are legitimate, while others are rip-offs, claiming to have lots of wonderful rental listings to get your money and then providing few if any. Before paying your money to any listing service use your common sense. If they promise results that sound too good to be true, they probably are.

If you feel that you have not received your money's worth from a rental listing service you do have some legal rights. Business & Professions Code 10167.9 states that prior to the acceptance of a fee from you the listing service must give you a written contract setting out your housing needs including type of unit (number of bedrooms, furnished or unfurnished, etc.), location, and the rent you are willing to pay. The service (unless they are a real estate broker) then has five days to come up with at least three available properties that match your specifications. If they don't, you are entitled to all of your money back if you ask for it within ten days following the five day period.

But what happens if you pay a rental listing service and then find a house some other way or don't find one at all? You are entitled to ask for your money back, whether you deal with a listing service or a real estate broker, except for a $25 service charge. You have ten days to make this demand in person or by mail after the contract expires.

If any listing service does not refund money you are entitled to, you can sue them in small claims court for the amount you paid plus $500 punitive damages. Punitive damages will be awarded if the rental service acted in bad faith.

B. LEARN ABOUT RENTAL AGREEMENTS

Before you start looking for a place, you should know a little about rental agreements.

NUMBER ONE RULE: Don't sign any papers until you understand what's in them, or you may regret it later. Reading these next few sections should help you to such an understanding, for, after all, there are only three different kinds of rental agreements, and all you really need to know is what they are like and the consequences to you of the different ones. If you know these few things you may be able to bargain for better terms, and you'll know better when to turn down an agreement altogether. If you read this chapter and still don't understand what's in your agreement, you should probably get some advice (see Chapter 1, Part C) before you make the deal.

THE THREE KINDS OF RENTAL AGREEMENTS

There are just three basic ways that residential rentals are commonly made: the Lease, the Written Rental Agreement and the Oral Rental Agreement. An oral agreement is made without anything being written down—you just talk over what the deal is and agree to it. The other two, the Lease and the Written Rental Agreement, have all the terms you agree to written down on a paper which you and the landlord sign.

1. ORAL AGREEMENTS

It is perfectly legal to make a deal orally—that is, without writing anything down, and no signatures. The landlord agrees to let you move in and you agree to pay a certain amount of rent on some schedule, like weekly, every other week or every month. The period between rent payments is what determines how much notice you are entitled to for rent raises or orders to get out. If you pay (a) weekly or (b) monthly, then you are entitled to (a) a week's or (b) 30 days notice.

The Oral Agreement has some advantages; it is relatively informal, you can move out on short notice, and you aren't subjected to the long list of terms and rules contained in most Leases and Written Rental Contracts. However, if you want the clarity of having everything written down, you may want your deal in writing, and if you want long-term security from rent raises and orders to move out because you do not live in a rent control city you will want a lease.

Oral agreements are legal, enforceable and have some advantages. But as time goes by and circumstances change, people's memories can have a funny habit of changing, too. Then, if something goes wrong, both sides end up in front of a judge who has to decide whom to believe. For this reason, even if you take an oral agreement, it may become very important to have some of the landlord's promises in writing. Therefore, if he promises to make repairs, return security deposits, or if he makes any other kind of deal with you that you want to make sure he remembers, then just ask him to write it down, date and sign it.

2. LEASES AND WRITTEN RENTAL AGREEMENTS

The Lease and the Written Rental Agreement are basically the same except for one terribly important difference:

THE LEASE fixes all the terms of the agreement so that no changes can be made for a given period of time—most commonly, one year. If you rent under a Lease, your rent cannot be raised until the Lease runs out nor can you be told to move unless you break the terms of the Lease. On the other hand, **you** can't easily get out of your obligations under the Lease until it runs out.

THE WRITTEN RENTAL AGREEMENT has everything written down, just like the Lease, but the time period is either indefinite, or else short—usually 30 days. This means that you can move out or your landlord can raise your rent or order you to move out on only 30 days' notice (sometimes less).*

Except for these very important differences, Leases and Written Rental Agreements are so much alike that they are sometimes hard to tell apart if you're not careful. Both of them cover the basic terms of rental (names, addresses, amount of rent and date due, deposits, etc.) and both of them tend to have a lot of other

---

*Several communities have modified this rule as part of their rent control to require "just cause" for eviction in certain circumstances. See Chapter 15.

fine print provisions to protect the landlord. When they are printed, they look alike, and the title at the top of the document can be misleading.

Legally, a written agreement can be typed or written down in longhand on any kind of paper, in any words, so long as the terms are understandable. However, as a practical matter, nearly all landlords use standard printed forms which they buy in stationery stores or get from landlord associations. These forms have been prepared by lawyers or real estate associations, and they are as favorable as possible to the landlord. These forms need not look like a death certificate, nor read like an act of Congress, but such is often the case. Some of the worst ones include clauses requring you to waive your privacy, accept shorter than normal notice periods for rent increases and termination, accept responsibility for fixing things that should be handled by your landlord and generally elevate the landlord into the position of a minor dictator. In the next section we discuss the common provisions and tell you some things to watch out for.

You will find a lease and rental agreement form fair to both landlord and tenant at the back of this book.

If the lease (for longer than a month) or month-to-month rental agreement is **negotiated** primarily **in Spanish,** then the landlord must give the tenant notice (in Spanish) of his right to request a Spanish translation of the lease or rental agreement.*

BE CAREFUL! Since they look so much alike, some forms can look like a lease, and sound like a lease, and even cover a year's period, but if they contain a provision that rent can be raised or that the agreement can be terminated on 30 days notice, then they are really only Written Rental Agreements.

READ IT CAREFULLY! It is **crucial** that you read the entire Lease and understand it before you sign it. If the Lease refers to another document such as "house rules" make sure you read a copy of these too. If there is any part of the written document that you don't understand, get advice (but not from the people who want you to sign the lease). If you want your rights protected, you will have to see to it yourself.

If the Lease offered to you by the prospective landlord is not satisfactory, it is legal and simple to change it if both parties can

---

*Civil Code Sec. 1632.

agree on the changes. All you do is cross out unwanted portions, write in desired changes, and have all parties who are going to sign the document initial the changes. Make sure that you sign the lease at the same time as the landlord and that you get a copy right away. Landlords have been known to make changes after you have signed the lease but before they have signed it.

ORAL PROMISES MAY NOT BE WORTH THE AIR IT TAKES TO MAKE THEM. Whenever there is a written agreement the law presumes that the parties wrote down **all** of the parts to it before they signed it. If the landlord makes promises which aren't written down, it is assumed they weren't made. Get everything you want included in writing before you sign.

3. COMMON PROVISIONS IN PRINTED FORMS AND WHAT TO WATCH OUT FOR

This section is about the fine print on the form agreements. There are probably hundreds of different printed forms and the provisions in them are all worded a little differently. It is often not at all obvious what some provisions mean (contrary to what form writers seem to think, it is **not** illegal to use plain English and be clear). We try to simplify the whole problem for you by setting out, in the list below, the most common kinds of printed form provisions, together with what they usually mean, and what to watch out for.

As will be seen, some of the provisions are illegal and therefore unenforceable. Since they are worthless, you should probably not waste your bargaining power by trying to get the landlord to scratch them out. It may sometimes help, however, to mention to him that these provisions are illegal, in order to show him how one-sided the agreement is, and then ask him to eliminate or change other (enforceable) provisions. There are some provisions which may be damaging to you later, so we advise you to try to get them out.

Whether you want to use your bargaining power on lease changes, however, rather than on trying to get repairs or a lower rent or lower security deposit, is a judgment you will have to make.

Many printed forms contain the following kinds of provisions:

a. Provision Against Assignment or Sub-lease Without Landlord's Consent

This prevents you from getting out of a lease by finding another tenant to take your place. Old cases say that a landlord's consent may be arbitrarily withheld, but newer cases* suggest that a landlord may not unnecessarily withhold his or her consent. In any case, you may want to try to get it scratched out or at least changed to state that the landlord cannot reject any new tenant that you find to replace you unless his credit or behavior is bad. In Chapter 7 we discuss how to get out of a lease even if the lease contains this sort of provision.

b. Provision That the Landlord is Not Responsible for Damage

This provision says that if the landlord is negligent in maintaining the place and you, your family, or your property is injured (for example, by falling down broken stairs), the landlord is not responsible for paying for your losses. This is called an "exculpatory" provision. Under Civil Code Section 1953 such a provision is invalid.

c. Waiver of Tenant's Rights under Civil Code Sections 1941 and 1942; or Making Tenant Responsible for Repairs

This provision requires the tenant to waive his rights under Civil Code Sections 1941 and 1942 to make repairs himself and deduct the cost from his rent. This waiver is not valid, so don't use up your bargaining power by making an issue of it.

The agreement might instead contain a provision requiring **you** to repair or maintain the premises. This provision does not relieve the landlord of his obligation **to the State** to see that the place complies with the housing codes. It might, however, stop you from exercising any rights **you** have (to repair and deduct, for example) against the landlord if he fails to make repairs. Therefore, try to get such a provision scratched out. Tell the landlord that the law imposes an obligation on **him** to make the place livable, and he should not try to pass this off on his tenants.

d. Waiver of Right to Legal Notice

This provision says the landlord can sue to evict you or can raise the rent or change the terms of the lease without giving any notice (such as a three day notice to pay your rent or vacate) required by

---

*See **In re Cox,** Cal. 3d 205 (1970) and 55 California State Bar Journal 108 (1980).

law. It is not valid. (Civil Code Section 1953.)

e. Provision Setting Notice Period

This provision sets the amount of time the landlord must give you before his notice of termination or rent raise or change in terms becomes operative. If there is no such provision, and you are a month-to-month tenant, the law requires that he give you 30 days notice. The law permits, however, such a provision to cut the notice period **down** to as low as **seven** days. This is very bad for you. If there is such a provision in the agreement, try to get it scratched out. Tell the landlord that you will need at least 30 days to find another place if he decides to terminate your tenancy or raise your rent.

f. Right to Inspect

Many forms have a provision which gives the landlord the right to come into your place to inspect it, or for other purposes.

Under a new statute, the landlord's right to enter the dwelling is limited to certain reasons, and any attempt to add to these reasons in the lease or rental agreement is void. See Chapter 6.

g. "Right of Re-entry" Provision

This provision permits the landlord to come in and throw you out if you don't pay the rent, without giving you legal notice of going to court. It is not valid.

h. Waiver of Jury Trial

This provision says that you waive your right to a trial by jury in any eviction law suit brought by the landlord. It is not valid.

i. Waiver of Right to Appeal

This provision prevents you from appealing a court decision in any eviction law suit. It is not valid.

j. Treble Damages

This provision says that if the landlord sues to evict you and wins, he may get not just the actual damages he has suffered (usually unpaid rent), but three times as much. The law provides for something very much like this anyway, so you might as well leave this provision alone.

k. Landlord's Attorney's Fees

This provision says that if the landlord has to sue to evict you or collect rent, you will pay his attorney's fees. This can amount to $150 to $300 or more. This provision is valid, and the landlord cannot get attorney's fees unless he has such a provision. Therefore, try to get it scratched out. If you lose your job or your welfare is cut off and you can't pay the rent, you don't want a judgment against you for attorney's fees in addition to back rent. (When you later get a job, the landlord can try to get this money taken out of your paycheck.)

Whenever you have such a provision, the law says that the attorney's fee provision entitles **you** to collect **your** attorney's fees from the landlord if you win the eviction law suit, even if the provision does not say this (C.C.P. Sec. 1717).

l. Late Charges

This provision requires the tenant to pay a late charge if he pays his rent late. The charge may be a percentage of the rent (such as 4%) or a flat fee (such as $10.00). This provision might be valid.* Try to get it scratched out, or at least have the landlord write that it doesn't apply if you cannot pay your rent on time for some good reason, such as delay in getting your paycheck or welfare check.

m. Entire Agreement

Somewhere in the fine print, usually at the end, most leases have a provision which says that the agreement is the **entire** agreement of the parties. That means that if the landlord made any promises which weren't written down, then they don't count and can't be enforced. It pays, under all circumstances, to get all promises from the landlord in writing.

4. WHICH IS BETTER, A LEASE OR A RENTAL AGREEMENT?

---

*Some court decisions indicate that late charge provisions might be successfully challenged. **Garrett v. South Coast Fed. S. I. L.,** 9 Cal. 3d 731 (1973); **Clermont v. Secured Investment Corp.,** 25 Cal. App. 3d 766 (1972); **Kirby v. Mann,** (San Mateo Muni. Ct., 1973) 78 Clearinghouse Review 685; 27 Stanford Law Review 1133 (1975).

If you have a lease for a substantial term, like a year or more, you are assured that the landlord cannot evict you or raise the rent so long as you pay your rent on time and meet your other obligations under the lease. This kind of security is extremely valuable in the situation where housing is hard to find and rents are rising, which, as you know all too well, describes the rental market in most California communities.

Of course, if you expect to be moving in a very short time, you may prefer a month-to-month rental agreement, so that you can leave simply by giving 30 days' notice. But don't be too sure that a month-to-month tenancy is what you want. In today's tight rental market, it is not usually difficult to "break" a lease if you have to. We discuss this possibility in Chapter 9. Basically, the rule is that, if you have a lease and move out before the term is up, the landlord can sue you for the rent as it comes due until the lease runs out, as long as he or she makes a reasonable effort to find another tenant. Because finding another tenant at the same rent or more is often so easy these days, there is normally little risk of loss in leaving before a lease runs out. (But see Chapter 9 for the details.)

All things being equal, a lease is commonly preferable to a rental agreement because it gives you security from rent increases and eviction. But if it is likely that you will be a very short term tenant, you will probably wish to rent under a written rental agreement, as getting out of a lease does involve some trouble.

The written rental agreement is often preferred by landlords. It gives them the right to raise the rent as often as they wish unless there is a local rent regulation ordinance, to get rid of tenants that they don't like, and to insert all sorts of clauses telling the tenant what he can't do. In most cases, from a tenant's point of view, the written rental agreement does not have the advantages of either a lease or an oral agreement.

On the other hand, the truth is that you often have to take what you can get.

5. MODEL LEASE AND MODEL RENTAL AGREEMENT

Most landlord's forms are very unfair. They impose many

requirements on the tenant and very few on the landlord. We offer a positive alternative for you to use, if you get the chance. Included at the back of the book are samples of two forms which are fair to both parties. They require the tenant to pay his rent and keep up his apartment while requiring the landlord to make repairs and not hassle the tenant. They leave out the harsh provisions found in most landlord's leases. Try to get your landlord to agree to use one of these forms instead o: his. Read the sections above to help you decide whether you want to use the Lease or the Rental Agreement.

Duplicate, ready-to-use copies of both these forms, plus two copies of the landlord/tenant checklist can be obtained by writing to Nolo Press, 950 Parker Street, Berkeley, CA 94710. Ask for the California Tenant Form Kit. The cost is $2.95. Sorry, it's not practical to send out forms one at a time.

C. SECURITY DEPOSITS, CLEANING FEES AND LAST MONTH'S RENT

Landlords usually require some type of deposit when they make a deal with a tenant. The landlord might call this deposit a "security deposit," "cleaning fee," or "last month's rent." Many tenants listen to such a label, do not really understand it, and then when they want to move out they don't know if they have a right to get the money back.

To avoid headaches later, you and the landlord must clearly understand at the outset what the deposit is for and when you can get it back. Once you reach this understanding, make sure to get it in writing, either as part of the rental document or in its own.

1. SECURITY DEPOSIT

When a landlord asks for a "security deposit," he usually wants some money to hold as security from loss of rent or damage to his property. If he requires you to clean the place before you leave, he wants security for costs of cleaning too. If you leave without paying rent or paying for breakage or cleaning the place properly, the landlord doesn't want to be bothered with finding you and suing you. He will just keep all or part of your security deposit.

Effective for all leases and oral and written rental agreements created or renewed on or after January 1, 1978 on residential property, the landlord is limited to collecting deposits or fees for cleaning when you leave, repair and non-payment of rent in an amount no greater than two months' rent if the property is unfurnished, and three months' rent if it is furnished. These amounts are in addition to any rent paid for the first month of occupancy, but include last month's rent paid in advance. Cal. Civil Code Section 1950.5.

As just noted the total amount that a landlord can charge for all types of deposits and fees is two times one month's rent if the place is unfurnished and three times if it is furnished. This means that if the rent is $300 per month and the apartment is not furnished, the landlord can charge up to a total of $600 for deposits and last month's rent.

When you move out, if you don't owe any rent, haven't broken anything, and have properly cleaned the place, the landlord must return your security deposit. If you do owe him something, he can keep what you owe him but must give you an itemized written statement as to what was retained and why and return the balance of your deposit. He must return whatever you have coming and give you the itemized statement within two weeks after you leave. If he refuses to return what you have coming, you can sue him to get it back. If you can also show that his refusal to return it was not because of some honest dispute but because he just wanted to cheat you, you might be able to collect "punitive damages" of up to $200 against him.*

---

*Civil Code Section 1950.5. See Chapter 8, Part B.

Some landlords have begun using companies which offer the landlord "protection" from bad tenants. Here's how it usually works: The landlord tells the tenant to see the company if the tenant doesn't want to put up the security deposit. The tenant pays the company a credit-check fee (sometimes as much as $50) **and,** if the tenant's credit is OK, a "protection fee" of about 15% of the security deposit. None of this is refundable, and note that if the tenant damages the premises, he **still** must pay for the damage (and cannot apply the "protection fee" to the cost of repairing the damage). This doesn't look like a very good deal for the tenant, to us.

In parts F and G below, we tell you some steps to take when you move in to make sure you get your deposit back, and, in Chapter 10, Part B, we discuss what to do when you move out to get your deposits back, and how to handle trouble at that time.

Cleaning deposits are just that, deposits that must be returned to the tenant when he or she moves out and leaves the place clean. Like security deposits, cleaning deposits are regulated under Section 1950.5 of the Civil Code. As noted above, a landlord can charge deposits (in addition to first month's rent, but including last month's rent) in an amount equal to twice one month's rent if a place is unfurnished, and three times one month's rent if it is furnished. This includes deposits and fees for cleaning, security and last month's rent. Thus, if a landlord charges you a $300 "security deposit" on an unfurnished flat that rents for $300 per month, he or she can charge an additional $300 for a "cleaning deposit," but can't charge for last month's rent.

But what about "fees" which the landlord claims to be "non-refundable"? For all tenancies commenced or renewed after January 1, 1978 (this includes all month-to-month tenancies), non-refundable fees are no longer legal except for very specific purposes which we discuss below. This means that, generally speaking, all fees and charges for cleaning, security and entering into a lease* are refundable and that, if they are not returned within two weeks of your moving out (unless the landlord has a valid reason for their retention), you can sue to get them back and may be able to recover an additional $200 in punitive damages.

There is one exception to this rule. It is set out in subsection (c) of Civil Code Section 1950.5 and says: "This subdivision shall not be construed to preclude a landlord and a tenant from entering into a mutual agreement for the landlord, at the request of the tenant and for a specified fee or charge, to make structural, decorative, furnishing or other similar alterations." The intent of this clause is clearly to compensate the landlord for strange or unusual alterations requested by the tenant, but there is a danger that some landlords may try to re-introduce "cleaning" or "security" type fees under it. Be awake to this possibility!

NOTE ON INTEREST ON SECURITY DEPOSITS:[**] While there is

---

*People v. Sangiacomo (1982) 180 Cal. Rptr. 594.
**A San Francisco ordinance requires landlords to pay tenants a minimum of 5% interest, but the regulation applies only to deposits held for at least a year. The cities of Berkeley and Santa Monica both have ordinances requiring that security deposits be put in an interest bearing account, and that the interest be returned to the tenant. Neither ordinance specifies a minimum allowable rate of interest.

no statewide requirement that landlords must pay tenants interest earned on their security deposits, a few cities now have ordinances requiring them to do so. Check to see if your city has enacted such an ordinance.

It would seem only fair to require this, since the money really belongs to the tenant (until he does something wrong and forfeits the deposit). No recent court decision has dealt with this problem, but in an older case, the court held that a landlord may not use or invest the tenant's security deposit.* If he does use it (i.e., does not keep it in a separate account, with interest going to the tenant), he is violating the rule in this case and should pay any profits he makes from the deposit—or at least interest at the legal rate—over to the tenant.** Note that our Model Lease and Model Rental Agreement forms—in the back of this book—expressly require the landlord to pay a moderate rate of interest on the security deposit.

3. LAST MONTH'S RENT***

Some landlords will ask that you pay the "last month's rent" in advance. This means just what it says—if you have a year's lease from January 1 to December 31, by paying "last month's rent" you are paying the rent for December in advance. If you have a month to month rental agreement, when you give notice that you are leaving in 30 days, your "last month's rent" will take care of your last month.

Landlords want "last month's rent" so that if you fail to pay your rent some month, they can treat that as the last month, evict you, and not lose any rent for that month.

The landlord **cannot** use the "last month's rent" as a security deposit for damage to the place. If he wants to collect for that sort of thing, he will have to sue you. Thus it is generally better for the tenant to pay "last month's rent" than a security deposit. (Best, of course, is paying none of these.)

If the tenant gives a security deposit and not last month's rent, he will have to pay the last month's rent when it comes due and

---

*Ingram v. Pantages, 86 Cal. App. 41 (1927). See also Legislative Counsel Opinion #4187 (3/3/75, to Senator Petris). Some local ordinances specifically allow landlords to invest security deposits, but require them to return the interest earned to their tenants.

Deposits," 26 U.C.L.A. L. Rev. 396 (1978).

***Section 1950.5 now states that effective for all tenancies commenced or renewed after January 1, 1978, all deposits taken together (including those for last month's rent) are limited to twice the monthly rental amount for unfurnished units and three times the monthly rental amount for furnished units.

then the **tenant** has to worry about how to get the security deposit back when he moves out. If the tenant pays only "last month's rent" in advance, the **landlord** has to worry about getting money from the tenant for any damages he claims. It's much better to have your money and let the other guy figure out how to get it, rather than the other way around.

4. "HOLDING" DEPOSIT

Sometimes if you make a deal with a landlord he will want some type of cash deposit, then and there, to make sure you don't change your mind and back out of the deal. If you give him the cash, sometimes as much as a month's rent, he will "hold" the place for you until you bring him your first month's rent and any deposits or fees you agreed on. This is called a "holding" or "bond" deposit.

If you give him a holding deposit and later decide not to take the place, you probably will be unable to get your deposit back. Therefore, be sure you really want the place before giving this kind of deposit.

Be sure you and the landlord understand what is to happen to the deposit when you take the place. Usually it will be applied to the first month's rent.* To make this clear, have the landlord give you a receipt for the deposit and have him write on the receipt what is to happen to the deposit when you come back with the rent.

5. CREDIT CHECK FEE

Landlords can, and often do, charge a fee to check the credit of prospective tenants. Credit checks normally cost no more than $25 and we believe that charging more is unreasonable. Some landlords have been known to take credit check fees from a number of tenants and pocket some or all of the money. Problems can also develop if the landlord takes a long time to check a tenant's credit and the tenant, not knowing whether or not the rental will be approved, rents another place. To avoid

---

*No case has dealt with this point yet, but it seems to be a fair reading of Civil Code Sec. 1950.5, which was intended to **limit** a landlord's use of deposits and advance payments, not expand it.

these and other possible areas of dispute, it is wise to sign a brief agreement with a landlord such as the following which is adapted from a model lease designed by some landlords and tenants in Berkeley, California.

CREDIT INFORMATION

Tenant authorizes Owner to verify all credit information for the purpose of renting the premises at (address). Owner shall not release such information for any other purpose without the express written approval of the Tenant.

If Owner/Agent does not agree to sign Lease within _____ days of receiving a deposit from Tenant for the purpose of reserving the premises, the total deposit shall be refunded to Tenant (less an amount to verify credit information).

Tenant may withdraw from the agreement and receive a refund of the total deposit (less an amount used to verify credit information) up until such time as Owner/Agent signs the lease.

_____ and _____
Landlord   Tenant

---

6. FINDER'S FEES

In some cities with rent control landlords are attempting to collect "finder's fees" that sometimes amount to as much as one or two months' rent. It works like this. When a prospective tenant applies to a landlord or management company they are told that they must either 1) pay a finder's fee directly to the landlord or management company to qualify to get a particular unit **or** 2) go to an apartment locator service and pay a finder's fee. In some situations the locator service will have been set up primarily to collect the fee and aren't really in the business of locating apartments.

This sort of fee is a refundable deposit if the tenant has found the unit and the locator organization has not provided any real service.* In cities with rent control, a phony locator fee may also violate the rent control ordinance. If you are asked for a finder's fee when you have already found the unit yourself (i.e. a friend moves out and tells you about it) and you live in a city with rent control, complain to:

---

*People v Sangiacomo (1982) 180 Cal.Rptr. 594.

- the consumer fraud division of your local district attorney's office;
- your city attorney;
- your local rent control or rent regulation board if one exists in your city.

If you live in a city without rent control, write the landlord a polite letter explaining that under the law the so-called "finder's fee" is actually a refundable deposit. Keep a copy of your letter. If you don't get the "finder's fee" back when you move out, you can file an action in small claims court (see Chapter 10(B)).

7. CREDIT REPORTS

A number of organizations such as Credit Fax in Northern California and U.D. Registry in Southern California, generally called consumer credit reporting agencies, collect information about tenants (this is most common in the L.A. area) such as whether they pay rent on time, were ever involved in an unlawful detainer action, etc. Larger landlords especially will routinely check with these agencies before renting to a prospective tenant. Civil Code Sections 1785.1-1786.4 require that if a landlord does not rent to a tenant, or charges more for a unit than otherwise would have been the case, because of information in a credit report, the tenant must be notified and told of the identity of the credit reporting agency. It also prohibits a credit agency from including any information about unlawful detainers where the tenant was adjudged the prevailing party. If the credit report is to discuss the tenant's character, general reputation, personal characteristics or mode of living, the tenant must be notified in writing within three days. In addition to these special protections tenants, like all consumers, are protected by the Fair Credit Reporting Act. If you believe a credit bureau or reporting agency may have given incorrect information about you to any creditor, including a landlord, you have a right to check. For detailed information see Chapter 4 of **Billpayers Rights** by Honigsberg & Warner (Nolo Press).

D. HOW TO CHECK A PLACE OVER

If you see a place that you think you will like, take a walk around the neighborhood. Check out where there are stores, schools and bus stops. Walk around the building you are interested in renting and try to meet some of the neighbors. Ask them how they have gotten along with the landlord. Make sure that you can feel at home in all respects. Take an especially close look at the condition of the unit you may rent. Look for dirt and damage, and carefully check all doors, windows, screens, stoves, furnaces, hot water heaters and any other appliances. Make lists of any defects you find—later you can negotiate with the land-lord for improvements and repairs. At the very least, be sure to get him to sign an acknowledgment of the existing conditions, so he can't blame you later for causing them.

In the section below we cover the landlord's responsibilities for the condition of the premises he rents. Then we show you exactly how to carefully check a place out to see if it meets legal standards.

1. HOUSING CODES AND ENFORCEMENT

Housing codes are laws which require a landlord to put his apartments and houses in good condition before renting them and to keep them that way while people are living there. The landlord cannot escape this duty by trying to impose it on the tenant in the lease or rental agreement.

California has a State Housing Law.* The main part of this law is contained in a little book called Uniform Housing Code. You can get a copy by sending a check or money order for $4.50 (plus tax) to International Conference of Building Officials, 5360 South Workman Mill Road, Whittier, California 90601. Repeated severe violations of the State Housing Law is a crime, punishable by a fine of up to $5,000 or imprisonment for up to one year, or both.**

Many cities and counties have also enacted housing codes. Local rules are at least as strict as the State Housing Law. Check with your City Clerk and County Clerk to see if you have such laws in your community.

The State Housing Law and local housing codes are enforced by local agencies. These are usually city and county Building Inspection Housing Departments. Other local agencies which might help you with certain health and housing conditions are the Health Department and Fire Department.

If you call a local agency such as a Building Inspection

---

*For a list of those conditions which violate the law see Health and Safety Code Section 17920.3.
**Health & Safety Code Section 17995.3. First time offenders face a fine of $500 and up to six months in jail or both, Health & Safety Code Section 17995.

Department and tell them that your landlord won't make repairs, they will send out a building inspector. He will inspect the place and make a report. If he finds housing code violations, he should send a letter to the landlord ordering him to make repairs. If he does not make them within a reasonable time, the inspector may order the building vacated until repairs are made, order the building demolished, or have the work done and charge the cost to the landlord.

In addition, **you** may be able to "enforce" the codes by suing the landlord, using rent money to make repairs, or withholding rent. These remedies are discussed in Chapter 7.

2. A CHECKLIST OF THINGS TO INSPECT

Here is a checklist of things you should look for when inspecting a place. All requirements mentioned are contained in the State Housing Law.

a. Check the STRUCTURE (floors, walls, ceiling, foundation).

The structure of the place must be weatherproof, waterproof and rodent proof.

"Weatherproof" means there must be no holes, cracks, or broken plaster. Check to see if all the walls are flush (that they meet directly, with no space in between). See if any floorboards are warped. Does wall plaster fall off when you touch it?

"Waterproof" means no water should leak in. If you see dark round spots on the ceilings or dark streaks on the walls, rain water might have been leaking through.

"Rodent proof" deals with cracks and holes which rats and mice could use.

b. Check the PLUMBING.

The landlord does not have to provide you with water, but he must provide a plumbing system connected to your community's water system and also to its sewage system (unless you have a cesspool).

All plumbing must be in a good condition, free of rust and leaks. Sometimes the condition of the plumbing is hard to discover, but there are several tests you can run to see if there might be problems.

Flush the toilet. Does it take too long to flush? Does it leak on the floor? Is the water discolored? If so, the pipes may be rusty or unclean.

If the water is connected, fill a sink with hot and cold water. Turn the faucets on all the way, and listen for vibrating or knocking sounds in the pipes. See if the water in the sink is discolored. Drain the sink, and see if it takes too long for the water to run out.

c. Check the BATHROOM.

The State Housing Law requires that every apartment and house have at least one working toilet, wash basin, and bathtub (or shower) in it. The toilet and bathtub (or shower) must be in a room which gives privacy to the occupant and which is ventilated. All of these facilities must be installed and maintained in a safe and sanitary condition.

d. Check the KITCHEN.

The State Housing Law requires that every apartment and house have a kitchen. The kitchen must have a kitchen sink, which cannot be made of wood or other absorbent material.

e. Check the HOT WATER.

The landlord must see that you have both hot and cold running water (although he can require you to pay the water and gas bills). "Hot" water means a temperature of not less than 120 degrees F.

f. Check the HEAT.

The landlord must provide adequate heating facilities. Unvented fuel-burning heaters are not permitted.

g. Check the LIGHT AND VENTILATION.

All rooms you live in must have natural light through windows or sky-lights, which must have an area not less than one-tenth of the floor area of the room, with a minimum of 12 square feet (3 square feet for bath-room windows). The windows must be openable at least half way for ventilation, unless mechanical ventilation is provided.

Hallways and stairs in the building must be lighted at all times.

h. Check for signs of INSECTS, VERMIN AND RODENTS.

The landlord must provide facilities to prevent insect and rodent infestation and, if there is infestation, provide for extermination services.

These pests can be hard to notice. Remember, however, that they are very shy and stay out of sight. Therefore, if you see any fresh **signs** of them, they are probably very numerous and will bother you later on. Also, these pests travel from house to house. If your neighbors have them, they will probably get to you.

Check for rodent trails and excrement. Rats and mice travel the same path day after day and leave a gray coloring along the floor and base-boards. Look at the kitchen carefully, for rodents go there for food supplies. Check in closets, cupboards, and behind appliances for cockroaches.

Check for possible breeding grounds nearby. Stagnant water is often a source of pests. So are garages and basements that have piles of litter or old couches.

As mentioned before, cracks and holes in the walls and floors can be entry-points for pests.

i. Check the WIRING AND ELECTRICITY.

Loose or exposed wiring can be dangerous, leading to shock or fires. The landlord must provide save and proper wiring.

If electrical power is available in the area, the place must be connected to it. Every room you live in must have at least two outlets (or one outlet and one light fixture). Every bathroom must have at least one light fixture.

j. Check for FIRE SAFETY.

The landlord must provide safe exits leading to a street or hallway. Hallways, stairways and exits must be free from litter. Storage rooms, garages, and basements must not contain combustible materials.

k. Check for adequate TRASH AND GARBAGE RECEPTACLES.

The landlord must provide adequate garbage and trash storage and removal facilities. Garbage cans must have tight-fitting covers.

l. Check the general CLEANLINESS OF THE AREA.

The landlord must keep those parts of the building which he controls (hallways, stairs, yards, basement, driveway, etc.) in a clean, sanitary, and safe condition.

3. WHAT IF THE PLACE DOES NOT MEET THE ABOVE STANDARDS?

If the place has serious problems, you should probably not rent it if you can possibly avoid it. A landlord who would even show you such a place probably won't or can't make the needed repairs. If the landlord promises to fix it up, be careful. First, ask other tenants how good the landlord is at keeping such promises. Second, make him put his promises in writing and sign it. Be sure he puts down **dates** on which certain repairs will be completed. Also, get him to write down that you will not have to pay your rent if he fails to meet the completion dates. If he doesn't want to agree to these things, he probably isn't taking his obligation to repair very seriously.

If you like the place but it has a few problems, simply ask the landlord to promise to make the necessary repairs. You might point out to him that he is required to do this before renting, under the State Housing Law, but you will rent the place and let him repair it later if he makes his promise (with dates) in writing and signs it.

If the landlord refuses to make the repaires, or if the place is so bad you don't trust his promises to make repairs, you should not rent the place, but you should report him to your city or county Building Inspection Department. He is violating the law (the State Housing Law), so this is your duty as a citizen. Also, you may be helping the tenant who ends up having to take the place.

E. HOW TO BARGAIN FOR THE BEST DEAL

Once you decide that you might like to rent a particular place you then negotiate the terms of the rental with the landlord or his agent. Often you will be presented with a "take it or leave it" proposition where the landlord is not open to making changes. Many times, however, landlords will be open to reasonable changes. Whether it be the rent that you are trying to change, or particular terms in the contract, it never hurts to try.

In your first negotiations it is good to remember that if the landlord is impressed with you he will be more likely to want you as a tenant. Take a moment to consider what sort of folks you would like to rent to if you were a landlord. In fact, you might think over the information in Chapter 1 about your landlord and his situation. Certainly, a good first impression can be made on the application form. Most landlords ask you to fill out an application listing your jobs, banks, cars, income and references. Be ready to make your application look as good as possible. Be coldly factual on information that the landlord can check easily and save exaggeration for those areas that can be checked only with difficulty. It's a good idea to photocopy your application. If you don't get the first place, it will be available to submit when you apply for other units.

How good a deal you can get from a landlord depends on how badly he wants you. If there are very few places available at the rent he is asking and a lot of people are looking, he may tell you to take his deal (rent, security deposit and form lease) or forget the whole thing. Even in such cases you may be able to squeeze a few concessions out of him which may save you money or hassles later on.

If there are lots of places for rent and not too many people looking, you will have more bargaining power. The landlord wants to rent the place soon (to get the rent) and may be afraid of losing you to another landlord.

Try to find out the situation before you bargain with a landlord. A good way is to see how long he has been trying to rent the place. Ask neighbors, or see how long he has had ads in the newspaper. If he has been trying for more than a month, he will be worried. If he has lowered the rent since he first started trying to rent it, he is really worried. Take advantage of it.

If you can, try to talk to the last tenant that lived in the place. He might give you some very valuable information about how to deal with the landlord, what is wrong with the place, and generally what it is like to live there. Other tenants or neighbors in the area might also be helpful on this.

The better you look as a responsible tenant, the more bargaining power you will have. Every landlord wants "responsible" tenants who will pay rent regularly, not mess up his place, and not complain about anything. The more you appear to be this way, the better the deal you will get. The landlord won't rent to you at all unless he trusts you, and if he trusts you, he may be willing to give you things you ask for in order to keep you.

If you have any bargaining power, try to use it. You are investing a lot of your money and energy for a long time to come, and you are entitled to shop around and bargain to get the best deal you can.

Some people don't like to bargain, because they think others will think they are cheap. But don't forget that the landlord is trying to get as much as he can out of his tenants, and he is not considered cheap, but a "good businessman." You should be a "good consumer" and get as much as you can for as little as you can get away with.

Even if the rent is fair and the landlord won't budge on that, there are other things he might give you if you ask. He may have a better refrigerator in storage or he may be willing to eliminate some lease provisions you don't like, or he may do some other things mentioned in this Handbook.

F. GET ALL PROMISES IN WRITING

Your future relationship with your landlord may be very pleasant. Hope for the best and try to be open, honest and friendly. However, at the same time, sensible steps should be taken for your own self protection just in case things take a nasty turn.

It often happens that a tenant moves into an apartment which has not been properly cleaned, or which needs painting or repairs. The landlord may say that the tenant can leave it in the same condition when he leaves, or perhaps that he can deduct money from the rent in exchange for cleaning, painting or repairs. whatever promises the landlord makes, you should be aware that it is very common for this sort of vague, oral agreement to lead to misunderstanding, bitterness and financial loss. The time to protect yourself is at the beginning. This may be your only chance to do so.

If a landlord promises to clean, paint, make repairs, reimburse you for material and work, or if there are any other kinds of promises you want to depend upon, get them in writing and put a date for completing the work. Asking for a promise in writing need not cause you tension or embarassment. Just tell the land- lord, politely, that you have made a simple list of what has been agreed to, and you want to go over it with him for clarification. If he agrees that the list is accurate, have him date and sign it. There should be two copies, one for the landlord and one for your own files.

The use of contracts is standard among business people and among friends when they are in a business relationship. The purpose of such writings is to remind people of what they once

agreed to do. If the landlord balks at putting things in writing, be very careful in all dealings with him.

Once the tenant moves in, it often takes landlords a long time to get around to doing promised work and if there is nothing in writing, sometimes the work never gets done. It is particularly important to get in writing any promise to reduce rent in exchange for material or your own labor. Every year thousands of landlords and tenants get into bitter disputes about this sort of agreement. It is not uncommon for the landlord's memory to get a little short after the work has been done.

If the landlord won't paint, clean or make repairs, be sure to list the faults as particularly and completely as you can and get him to sign and date the list. Otherwise he may later claim that you caused the damage.

January 1, 19____

Landlord *Smith Realty* and Tenant *Patricia Parker* make the following agreement:

1. Patricia Parker agrees to buy paint and painting supplies not to exceed a cost of $120 and to paint apartment #4 at 1500 Acorn Street, Cloverdale, California, on or before February 1, 19____ and to forward all receipts for painting supplies and paint to Smith Realty;

2. Smith Realty agrees to reduce the payment due February 1, 19____ by $150 in consideration for the painting to be done by Patricia Parker and in addition to allow Patricia Parker to deduct the actual cost of paint and painting supplies (not to exceed $120) from the rent payment due February 1, 19____.

3. The premises are being rented with the following defects:
   a. dent in oven door,
   b. gouge over fireplace in wall.

Smith Realty Company
By: B. C. Smith

Patricia Parker

G. SELF PROTECTION WHEN MOVING IN

When you are about to move in, take a look around. If there is anything at all wrong with the place—if there is any dirt or damage of any kind—get a few of the most responsible of your friends to take a look at it. This is so that, if necessary, they can later testify to the condition of the place when you moved in. Get them to write a simple little dated note (reminder) of what they saw. If at all possible, have a friend take a photograph of all defects. When developed, properly identify each photo on the back by location, date and signature. All notes and pictures should go into your file with your other records.

If you plan to attach cupboards, shelves, bookcases, air conditioners, room dividers or anything at all to the premises, you should get something in writing from the landlord permitting you to install such things, and (if you plan it) to later remove them. By California law, anything which is nailed, screwed or bolted to the premises becomes the property of the landlord. If you remove the object when you leave, your landlord will have the right to recover compensation for any damages suffered to the premises and may also be able to recover the value of the object removed unless there is a written agreement to the contrary. In addition, most landlords are sensitive about having the premises altered without their consent and may get quite irritated if they discover changes after they have already been made.

1. LANDLORD-TENANT CHECKLIST

Another good self-protection device for both landlord and tenant involves taking an inventory of the condition of the premises at the time you move in, and then again when you move out. This means no more than making a brief written record of the condition of each room and having it signed by you and your land-lord. Not only does the inventory give both of you an accurate record of the condition of the unit, but the act of making it provides a framework for communication and the resolution of potential disputes.

When filling out your checklist you will want to be as specific as possible. Thus you might state next to stove and refrigerator:

"generally good, but oven greasy and refrigerator dirty." Be sure to note things like worn rugs, chipped enamel, holes in screens, dirty cabinets, etc. If you need more space than provided on your checklist form, make a separate writing for those items signed by both landlord and tenant and have it stapled to the checklist. You will find a sample checklist at the back of this book. Make two copies so that both you and your landlord each have a signed copy.

H. YOUR RESPONSIBILITIES AS A TENANT

1. COMPLY WITH YOUR LEASE OR RENTAL AGREEMENT

Your most important responsibility as a tenant is to comply with the provisions of your lease or rental agreement. If you do not, you may have to pay money to the landlord or you may be evicted, and sometimes both. Read your lease or agreement carefully to see what it requires you to do and prevents you from doing.

2. PAY YOUR RENT ON TIME

You must pay your rent on the day it is due. Most leases and rental agreements say rent is due on the first of the month. However, if the first falls on a Saturday or Sunday or a legal holiday, then the law says that the rent can be paid on the next business day.*

If you do not pay your rent on time, you may have to pay a late charge, if your lease or rental agreement provides for this. Also, your landlord may serve upon you a "three-day notice" to pay your rent in three days or get out. If you do not comply with the three-day notice, he can then sue to evict you.

---

*Code of Civil Procedure Section 13; Government Code Section 6700 et seq.

You are entitled to a written receipt whenever you pay your rent.* Be especially sure to get one if you don't pay by check, as this is proof that you paid your rent. Keep your receipts in a safe place—preferably in the file that you set up for all documents relating to the rental transaction.

3. KEEP THE PLACE CLEAN

The housing codes and almost all agreements require that you keep your place clean, safe and sanitary. You must properly dispose of all garbage and trash in your premises, placing it in the containers provided by the landlord.

4. REPAIR ANYTHING YOU BREAK

Anything damaged by you, other occupants or guests must be repaired at your expense, **unless** the damage resulted from "normal wear and tear" during ordinary use., If you sit on a chair and it breaks from old age, you do not have to repair or replace it. If, however, your child breaks the chair in a temper tantrum, you must pay for it.

I. CO-SIGNING LEASES

Some landlords have begun requiring a co-signor on leases and rental agreements as a condition of renting. Normally, they ask the co-signor to sign a contract saying that he will pay for any rent or damage losses that the tenants fail to pay. Several landlords have told us that inclusion of this sort of provision is mostly psychological and that they don't often sue the co-signor even if the original tenant defaults. Psychological or not, it is possible that a co-signor will be sued if the tenant defaults, so don't co-sign if

---

*Civil Code Section 1499: "A debtor has a right to require from his creditor a written receipt for any property delivered in performance of his obligation."

you are not fully ready to pay.

IMPORTANT: Many co-signor clauses don't appear to be enforceable in court because they are so vague that they don't qualify as contracts. If a landlord and tenant change the terms of their rental agreement without the approval of the co-signor, he or she is no longer responsible.* Of course defenses that a tenant may raise (e.g., breach of the warranty of habitability) may be raised by the co-signor. (See Chapter 3.)

---

*See also Civil Code Section 2819; **Wexler v. McLucas,** 48 CA3 Supp. 9 (1975).

3
SHARING A HOME

It's more and more common for two or more unmarried people to rent a place together. Commonly a sexual relationship forms the basis of the decision to share, but often it does not. But whether or not it involves sharing a bed, sharing a home can have all sorts of legal ramifications. Of course, there are legalities when it comes to dealing with the landlord, but sometimes the legal rules governing the relationship between the roommates are of even more importance.

A. IS IT LEGAL TO LIVE TOGETHER?

The answer is yes when two adults live together. And it makes no difference whether they are gay or straight, if one or both is married to someone else, or if they have or don't have a sexual relationship. There used to be laws against gay sexual conduct and against people living together when married to someone else, but since 1976 these laws no longer exist in California. Does the repeal of these laws mean that landlords must rent to gay couples or unmarried couples? Not directly, but there are other state and local laws banning certain types of discrimination (see Chapter 5).

Three or more people used to have trouble setting up house-keeping together, even if they are all as celibate as nuns. Why? Because some communities had local zoning ordinances banning more than two (sometimes the number was set at three or four) unrelated persons from living together (excepting household help, of course). Usually these ordinances were in effect in con-servative communities which are uptight about what they see to be "hippie communes." While many legal scholars feel that such ordinances discriminate against unmarried persons and should be ruled unconstitutional throughout the country in that they deny equal protection of the laws to such persons, the United States Supreme Court does not agree. In the case of **Village of Belle Terre v. Boraas**, 416 U.S. (1974), the Supreme Court held that anti-group living ordinances are constitutional. However, the California Supreme Court has ruled that this sort of ordinance is unconstitutional under the California Constitution and thus local ordinances barring more than two unrelated people from living together are not enforceable in California.* This means that three or more unrelated people can live together anyplace in California, but if they move out of the state, they could be barred by local ordinances in other areas.

B. THE LEGAL OBLIGATIONS OF ROOMMATES TO THE LANDLORD

If two people—let's call them Ted and Carol—enter into a lease or rental agreement (written or oral), they are each on the hook to the landlord for **all** rent and **all** damages to the apart-ment (except "normal wear and tear"). It makes no difference who (or whose friends) caused the damage, or who left without paying the rent. Let's look at several common situations.

EXAMPLE 1: Ted and Carol both sign a written rental agree-

---

*City of Santa Barbara v. Adamson, 164 Cal. Rptr. 539 (1980).

ment providing for a total monthly rent of $600 for a flat. They agree between them to each pay one-half. After three months Ted refuses to pay his half of the rent (or moves out with no notice to Carol and the landlord). In either situation, Carol is legally obligated to pay all the rent, as far as the landlord is concerned. Ted, of course, is equally liable, but if he is unreachable or out of work, the landlord will almost surely come after Carol for the whole amount. Snce Ted and Carol have rented under a month-to-month written rental agreement, Carol can cut her losses by giving the landlord a 30 day written notice of intention to move. She can do this even if Ted is lying around the place, refusing to pay or get out.

IMPORTANT: If Carol ends up paying the landlord more than her agreed share of the rent, she has a right to recover from Ted. If payment is not made voluntarily, Carol can sue Ted in Small Claims Court.*

EXAMPLE 2: The same fact situation as Example 1, except that this time there is a lease for one year. Again, both partners are independently liable for the whole rent. If one refuses to pay, the other is still liable unless a third person can be found to take over the lease, in which case both partners are off the hook from the day that a new tenant takes over. As we discuss in Chapter 10, because of the housing shortage in most parts of the state, it is often easy for a tenant to get out of a lease at little or no cost, by simply finding an acceptable new tenant and steering him or her to the landlord. A newspaper ad will usually do it. The landlord has an obligation to limit his or her damages (called "mitigation of damages" in legal lingo) by renting to a suitable new tenant as soon as possible. Should the landlord fail to do this, he/she loses the legal right to collect damages from the original tenants.

C. THE LEGAL OBLIGATIONS OF ROOMMATES TO EACH OTHER

People sharing a home usually have certain expectations of each other. Sometimes it helps to write these down. After all, you expect to write things down with the landlord almost as a matter of course, so why not do the same with each other? Nothing that Carol and Ted agree to among themselves has any effect as far as

---

*See **Everybody's Guide to Small Claims Court,** Warner, Nolo Press.

the landlord is concerned, but it still may be helpful to have something to refresh their memories, especially if the relationship gets a little rocky. Here we have a sample agreement. Of course there are many other terms that could be included in this type of agreement and you will probably wish to make some modifications.*

AGREEMENT

Carol Pladsen and Ted Kutrumbos, upon renting an apartment at 1500 Redwood Street, #4, Philo, California agree as follows:

1. Carol and Ted are each obligated to pay one-half of the rent and one-half of the utilities, including the basic monthly telephone charge. Each person will keep track of and pay for his or her long distance calls. Rent shall be paid on the first of each month, utilities within ten days of the day the bill is received.

2. If either Carol or Ted wants to move out, the one moving will give the other person 30 days' notice and will pay his/her share of the rent for the entire 30 day period even if he/she moves out sooner. If both Carol and Ted wish to move, they will be jointly responsible for giving the landlord 30 days' notice.

3. No third persons will be invited to stay in the apartment without the mutual agreement of both Carol and Ted.

4. If both Carol and Ted want to keep the apartment but one or the other or both no longer wishes to live together, they will have a third party flip a coin to see who gets to stay. The loser will move out within 30 days and will pay all of his/her obligations for rent, utilities and for any damage to the apartment.

Here is an alternative for number 4.

4. If both Carol and Ted want to keep the apartment but no longer wish to live together, the apartment shall be retained by the person who needs it most. Need shall be determined by taking into consideration the relative financial condition of each party, proximity to work, the needs of minor children, if any, and

---

*If you are interested in a comprehensive living together agreement, see **The Living Together Kit,** Ihara & Warner, Nolo Press.

(list any other factors important to you). The determination shall be made by a third party (the arbitrator) who both Carol and Ted agree in writing is objective. If it is impossible to agree on an arbitrator, the arbitrator will be chosen by (fill in name). The arbitrator shall be paid $35 per hour. The determination shall be made within ten days after either party informs the other that he or she wishes to separate, and after the arbitrator has listened to each person present his or her case. The arbitration award shall be conclusive on the parties, and shall be prepared in such a way that a formal judgment can be entered thereon in any court having jurisdiction over the dispute if either party so desires. After the determination is made, the person who is to leave shall have an additional ten days to do so. The person who leaves is obligated for all rent, utilities and any damage costs for 30 days from the day that the original determination to separate is made.

Date   Carol Pladsen

Date   Ted Kutrumbos

D. HAVING A FRIEND MOVE IN

Perhaps just as common as two or more people renting a home together is for one person to move into a place already rented and occupied by another. This is often simple and smooth when the landlord is cooperative, but can raise some tricky legal questions if the landlord raises objections.

In some situations where the landlord is not in the area or is not likely to make waves, it may be sensible to simply have the second person move in and worry about the consequences later. But is this legal? Is a tenant required to tell his landlord when a second person moves in? It depends on the lease or rental agreement. If no mention is made as to the number of persons allowed in the apartment, use your own discretion and knowledge of your land-lord. Some don't care, but most probably do. We suspect that as a general rule, moving someone in without the consent of a land-lord is not the most sensible thing to do. The landlord will probably figure out what is going on before long and may resent your sneakiness more than he or she resents your roommate. We advise you to:

- Read the lease or rental agreement to see how many people are allowed to live on the premises and if there are any restrictions. Sometimes additional people will be allowed for a slight increase in rent. Many landlords will not care whether you are married, living together or joined by the toes with rubber bands, but will expect to collect more money if more people live in their rental unit.
- Contact the landlord to explain what is happening. If you can't do this in person, you might send a letter such as this:

1500 Redwood Street #4
Philo, California
June 27, 19____

Smith Realty
10 Ocean Street
Elk, California

Dear Sirs:

I live at the above address and regularly pay rent to your office. As of July 1, 19____, there will be a second person living in my apartment. As set forth in my lease, I enclose the increased rent due which now comes to a total of $450. I will continue to make payments in this amount as long as two people occupy the apartment.

Should you wish to sign a new lease to specifically cover two people, please let me know. My friend, Carol Pladsen, is regularly employed and has an excellent credit rating.

Very truly yours,

Ted Kutrumbos

REMEMBER: Under state law, a written rental agreement may be terminated on thirty days' notice without the necessity of the landlord giving a reason.* Thus, a landlord who wants to get rid of you can normally do so without too much trouble if you don't have a lease. So it pays to be reasonable when moving roommates in and out.

If you have a lease, you are probably in a little better position to bargain with the landlord if a friend moves in. This is because, to get you out before the lease expires, he would have to establish that you have violated one or more lease terms. If your lease has a provision allowing occupancy by only one person, your landlord probably has the right to terminate your tenancy if a second person moves in without his permission. However, if the landlord accepts rent with the knowledge that you are living with someone, many courts would hold that he can no longer enforce that right. Of course, if you cause the landlord too much grief, he can simply refuse to renew your lease when it runs out. Again, you will probably come out ahead by being reasonable and cooperative.

1. WHAT IS THE LEGAL RELATIONSHIP BETWEEN THE PERSON MOVING IN AND THE LANDLORD?

If Carol moves into Ted's apartment, what is the relationship between Carol and Ted's landlord? Is Carol obligated to pay rent if Ted fails to pay? What if Ted moves out, but Carol wants to remain? If Ted ruins the paint or breaks the furniture, does Carol have any obligation to pay for the damage?

The answer to these questions is that Carol starts with no legal rights or obligations to the landlord (but possibly to Ted) regarding the rent, or the right to live in the apartment. She has entered into no contract with the landlord.** Ted is completely liable for the rent and also for damage to the premises whether caused by Carol or himself, because he has entered into a contract which may be in the form of a lease, written rental agreement or

---

*In several populous areas, including San Francisco, Los Angeles, Berkeley, and Santa Monica (see Chapter 15 for a complete list), this rule has been changed by local rent control ordinances which prevent evictions except for reasons specified in the various enactments. These "just cause" for eviction rules are discussed in Chapter 15. Also, the eviction can't be for a type of discrimination prohibited under California law (see Chapter 6).

**Of course, if she damages the property, she is liable just as a visitor, a trespasser, or a thief who caused damage would be liable.

oral rental agreement. If Ted leaves, Carol has no right to take over his lease without the landlord's consent.

Carol can, of course, enter into a lease or rental agreement contract with the landlord which would give her the rights and responsibilities of a tenant. This can be done by:

- Signing a new lease or rental agreement which specifically includes both Ted and Carol as tenants.
- Making an oral rental agreement with the landlord. Be careful of this one, as an oral agreement can consist of no more than a conversation between Carol and the landlord in which she says she will pay the rent and keep the place clean and he says OK. There may be some legal question as to whether an oral agreement between Carol and the landlord is enforceable if there is still a written lease or rental agreement between the landlord and Ted which doesn't include Carol, but it is our belief that most judges would bend over backwards to give Carol the rights and responsibilities of a tenant if she seemed to be exercising them.
- The actual payment of rent by Carol and its acceptance by the landlord, especially if it is done on a fairly regular basis. As in the preceding paragraph, this would set up a month-to-month tenancy between Carol and the landlord and would mean that either could end the tenancy by giving the other a 30 day written notice of intention to end the tenancy.

Should the situation ever arise that Ted wants to move out and Carol remain, it is important that the legal relationships be clarified. Ted should give the landlord a written notice of what he intends to do at least 30 days before he leaves. If he does this, he is off the hook completely in a written or oral rental agreement situation. If a lease is involved and Ted is leaving before it runs out, he might still be OK, because the landlord has a legal duty to take steps to limit his loss as much as possible (mitigate damages—see Chapter 9). This means finding a new tenant to pay the rent. In our example, as long as Carol is a reasonably solvent and non-destructive person, the landlord would suffer no loss by accepting her as a tenant to fill out the rest of Ted's lease. If the landlord refuses Carol without good reason, Ted will probably be legally absolved of future responsibility and any loss is legally the land-lord's problem, not his (see Chapter 9 for details).

(For use if you have a rental agreement)

1500 Redwood Street #4
Philo, California
June 27, 19____

Smith Realty
10 Ocean Street
Elk, California

Dear Sirs:

I live at the above address and regularly pay rent to your office. On July 31, 19____ I will be moving out. As you know, my friend, Carol Pladsen, also resides here. She wishes to remain and will continue to pay rent to your office on the first of each month.

We will be contacting you soon to arrange for the return of my damage deposits of $300, at which time Carol will give you a similar deposit. If you have any questions, or if there is anything we can do to make the transition easier for you, please let us know.

Very truly yours,

Ted Kutrumbos

(For use if you have a lease)

1500 Redwood Street #4
Philo, California
June 27, 19____

Smith Realty
10 Ocean Street
Elk, California

Dear Sirs:

I live at the above address under a lease which expires on October 30, 19____. A change in my job makes it necessary that I leave the last day of February. As you know, for the last six months my friend, Carol Pladsen, has been sharing this apartment. Carol wishes either to take over my lease or enter into a new one with you for the remainder of my lease term. She is employed, has a stable income, and will, of course, be a responsible tenant.

We will soon be contacting your office to work out the details of the transfer. If you have any concerns about this proposal, please give us a call.

Very truly yours,

Ted Kutrumbos

2. WHAT IS THE LEGAL RELATIONSHIP BETWEEN THE PERSON MOVING IN AND THE PERSON ALREADY THERE?

Alas, it seems all too common that big-brained monkeys go through violent changes in emotional feelings. A relationship that is all sunshine and roses one minute may be more like a skunk cabbage in a hurricane the next. Sometimes, when feelings change, memories blur as to promises made in happier times and the nicest people become paranoid and nasty. Suddenly, questions such as "whose apartment is this, anyway?" may turn into serious disputes. We suggest that when feelings are relaxed (preferably at the time that the living arrangement is set up), both people make a little note as to their mutual understandings, either as part of a comprehensive living together arrangement or in a separate agreement. If this is done in a spirit of making a writing to aid the all too fallible human memory, it need not be a heavy experience. We include here an example that you might want to change to fit your circumstances.

AGREEMENT

Carol Pladsen and Ted Kutrumbos make the following agreement:

1. Ted will move into Carol's apartment and will give Carol one-half of the monthly rent ($300) on the first of each month. Carol

will continue paying the landlord under her lease and Ted will have no obligation under the lease.

2. Ted will pay one-half of the electric, gas, water, garbage and monthly telephone service charges to Carol on the first of each month; Carol will pay the bills.

3. Should Ted wish to move out, he will give Carol as much written notice as possible and will be liable for one-half of the rent for two weeks from the time he gives Carol written notice. Should Carol wish Ted to move out, she will give him as much written notice as possible, in no case less than two weeks. In any case of serious dispute, it is understood that Carol has first choice to remain in the apartment and Ted must leave on her request.

Date   Carol Pladsen

Date   Ted Kutrumbos

IMPORTANT: If you get into a serious dispute with your friend involving your shared home and have no agreement to fall back on, you will have to do the best you can to muddle through to a fair solution. Here are a few ideas to guide your thinking.

- If only one of you has signed the agreement with the landlord and that person pays all the rent, then that person probably should have the first claim on the apartment, especially if that person occupied the apartment first. The other should be given a reasonable period of time to find another place, especially if he or she has been contributing to the rent and/or has been living in the home for any considerable period of time.
- If you have both signed a lease or rental agreement and/or both regularly pay rent to the landlord, your rights to the apartment are probably legally equal, even if one of you got there first. Try to talk out your situation, letting the person stay who genuinely needs the place the most. Some people find it helpful to set up an informal arbitration proceeding with a neutral third person who will listen to the facts before making a decision. If you do this, make sure that the arbitrator is not a close friend, as the

person who loses is likely to have hard feelings. Lean over backwards to be fair about adjusting money details concerning such things as last month's rent and damage deposits. Allow the person moving out a reasonable period of time to find another place. **We have found that the best compromises are made when both people feel that they have gone more than half way.**

- Each person has the right to all his or her belongings. This is true even if they are behind in his or her share of the rent. Never lock up the other person's property.
- It is a bad idea to deny a person access to his or her home except in the most extreme circumstances. If you are going to lock out a person, you should also be ready to sign a formal police complaint because it may come to that if your former friend tries to get in by using force. In most cases, locking out a person is not legal and you can be sued for damages.

E. GUESTS

What about overnight guests—particularly those who stay over often? What relationship if any do these people have with the landlord? More important, is the landlord entitled to any legal recourse if you have a "regular" guest?

There is no precise line between guests and roommates. A person may be a frequent overnight visitor—four or five times a week—but still qualify as a guest, whereas a roommate may only be in residence a couple of days a week, as is common with flight attendants. A person's status as guest might be considerably enhanced by a showing that he or she maintains a separate residence complete with furniture and mailing address. However, to the landlord who sees the person on the premises more than the actual tenant, this might not prove persuasive.

Where the landlord is seeking to evict on the basis of a lease provision which prohibits occupancy of more than a certain number, he or she must prove that the extra occupant is in fact a resident. However, as we mentioned earlier in this chapter (Section D), in many parts of the state the landlord can evict for no reason at all if you have no lease. For this reason, therefore, unless you live in an area covered by a "just cause" for eviction ordinance (see Chapter 15), or have a lease, it might be a good idea to clarify your guest's status with your landlord at the outset instead of leaving things to his or her imagination.

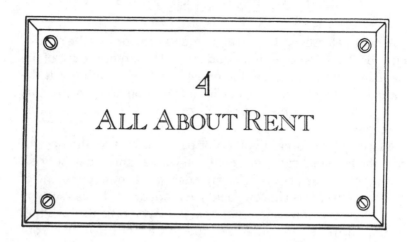

4
ALL ABOUT RENT

A. HOW MUCH CAN
THE LANDLORD CHARGE?

Under California law the landlord can charge you as much rent as he or she can get, as there is no statewide rent regulation law. However, it is legal for cities and counties to pass their own rules to limit rent increases. A number have done so, but most have not (see Chapter 15).

If you live in **public** housing, the rent can be no more than 25% of your income, **after** certain deductions are taken. The same is true if you live in private housing under the "leased housing" or "Section 8" program run by your local housing authority.* This is one reason why many people try hard to get into public housing or leased housing. If you don't know whether there are such programs in your community, call City Hall or the County Administration Building.

---

*In some circumstances people with higher incomes (over 50% of the area median) must pay 30% of their income under the leased housing program. Contact the U.S. Department of Housing and Urban Development (HUD) for details.

Needless to say, try to bargain a private landlord down on the rent he is asking, if you think you can.

B. WHEN IS RENT DUE?

Almost all leases and rental agreements provide that the rent for a period is due before the period starts. Thus, rent for use of the place in March would be due on March 1. Although this is the common practice, California Civil Code Section 1947 provides that rent is due at the end of the term, unless the parties agree otherwise.

As we will see later, if you don't pay your rent on the day it is due, the landlord can then serve you with a "three-day notice," telling you to pay your rent in three days or get out. At the end of the three days, if you haven't paid your rent or left, he can sue you and get an eviction order, court costs, maybe his attorney's fees and up to three times the rent due (if he can prove that your refusal to vacate the premises was deliberate and intended).

If you run into trouble paying your rent on time, three days isn't much time to come up with it. You might expect such trouble if your income is from alimony and child support, welfare, or a job which might involve lay-offs or strikes. If this might happen to you, ask the landlord to put in the lease or rental agreement a provision that he will not serve a "three-day notice" on you until some time (like ten days or twenty days) after the first of the month. If he objects, write the provision so that it gives you the extra time only if your income is temporarily cut off or delayed, and maybe he will accept that.

If for any reason your landlord refuses to accept your rent you can best protect yourself by opening a bank account in your landlord's name and depositing the correct amount [Civil Code Section 1500].

C. CALIFORNIA RENT LAW

Under California law, rent cannot be raised during a **lease** unless the written terms of the lease itself specifically allow the increase. Rent can be increased under a written or oral rental agreement if proper written notice is given to the tenant (the various rental agreements are described fully in Chapter 2, Part B). Where rent is paid monthly, written notice must be given at least 30 days prior to the increase.* Oral notice of rent increases is not legally sufficient. California law allows a landlord renting under an oral or written agreement to raise the rent as much as he wishes in most circumstances. The main exceptions to this rule are that:

1. The landlord cannot raise the rent at any time to retaliate against the tenant for becoming involved with a tenant organization, or for any other exercise of a tenant's legal rights;

2. The landlord cannot raise the rent to retaliate against the tenant's reporting code violations to a city agency or using his repair-and-deduct remedy to fix defects (see Chapter 7), for 180 days after either of these things happen.**

3. More restrictive rules on when rent can be raised are in force in several cities and counties that have enacted local rent control ordinances. See Chapter 15.

It has been our experience that most landlords simply **mail** notice of rent increases to their tenants. Under California law, this is **not** proper service of the notice. The notice must be served as follows: (1) by handing it to the tenant personally, or (2) **if** the tenant is absent from home and work, by leaving the notice with "a person of suitable age and discretion" at home or work, **and** mailing a copy to the tenant, or (3) **if** the landlord cannot find out where the tenant lives and works, or a person of suitable age and discretion cannot be found, then the landlord may complete the service by doing all three of these things—posting the notice in a conspicuous place on the property, leaving a copy with someone residing in the rented premises (if such person can be found), and mailing a copy to the tenant.***

D. RENT CONTROL

See Chapter 15.

---

*Civil Code Section 827
**Civil Code Section 1942.5
***Civil Code Section 827, Code of Civil Procedure Section 1162.

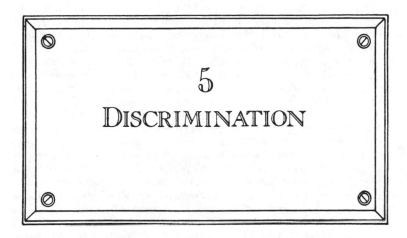

5
DISCRIMINATION

There was a time when a landlord could refuse to rent to just about anyone he didn't like. All sorts of groups—including blacks, Asians, Chicanos, women, unmarried couples, gays and many more—were routinely subjected to discrimination. Fortunately, our state and federal legislatures have taken steps to end these abuses, and many more forms of discrimination have been made unlawful.

It is illegal for a landlord to refuse to rent to you or engage in any other kind of discrimination on the basis of a group characteristic which is not closely related to the legitimate needs of the landlord. A combination of statutes and cases forbid discrimination on the following grounds:

- Race
- Religion
- Ethnic Background
- Sex
- Marital status (includes discrimination against unmarried couples)
- Physical Disability
- Families with children (unless the rental units are specifically designated for older citizens as is the case with retirement communities)

*Racial discrimination is forbidden by California Health and Safety Code Sections 35720 et seq. (Govt. Code 12900 et seq.); California Civil Code Sections 51 and 52 (Unruh Civil Rights Act); the Civil Rights Act of 1866 (see **Jones v. Alfred H. Meyer Co.,**) 392 U.S. 409 [1968]); and by 42 U.S. Code Sections 3601 et seq. (Fair Housing Act of 1968). Religious and ethnic discrimination are forbidden by all of the above except the Civil Rights Act of 1866. Sex discrimination is forbidden by California Civil Code Sections 51 and 52 and by the Federal Fair Housing Act of 1968. Physical disability discrimination is forbidden by California Civil Code Section 54.1. Marital status discrimination includes discrimination against unmarried couples, **Atkinson v. Kern County Housing Authority,** 58 Cal. App. 3d 89 (1976). Discrimination on the basis of age (including discrimination against children) is forbidden by Civil Code Sections 51 and 52, unless the requirements of Civil Code Section 51.3 authorizing specially designed accessible housing for senior citizens are met. These require either new construction or the substantial renovation of existing housing for senior citizens. Detailed rules as to who qualifies to live in senior housing depend on whether the housing is considered a "senior citizen housing development." If so, one spouse or cohabitant must be 62 years of age. In other designated senior housing at least one spouse or cohabitant must be 55 years of age. In both instances, exceptions are made for people who provide primary physical care to seniors and temporary residents of 60 days or less per calendar year. Also see **Marina Point, Ltd. v. Wolfson,** 100 Cal. Rptr. 496 (1982). Discrimination against homosexuals is forbidden by **Hubert v. Williams** (1982) 184 Cal. Rptr. 161. In addition, several cities and counties can help you enforce your rights, as they have passed local ordinances barring discrimination against gays. These include Berkeley, San Francisco, Los Angeles and San Mateo County.

■ ■ ■

In addition, the California Supreme Court has held that state law forbids landlords from **all** arbitrary discrimination. The Court indicated that discrimination against the following groups would be arbitrary: Republicans, students, welfare recipients, "entire occupations or avocations, e.g., sailors or motorcyclists," and "all nonhomosexuals."*

A. HOW TO TELL IF A LANDLORD IS DISCRIMINATING

Occasionally an apartment house manager—and rarely a landlord himself—will tell you that he will not rent to blacks, Spanish-surnamed people, Asians, etc. This does not happen often any more, because these people are learning that they can be penalized if it is proved that they are discriminating.

Marina Point, Ltd. v. Wolfson (1982) 30 Cal. 3d 721.

Today, most landlords who wish to discriminate try to be subtle about it. When you phone to see if a place is still available, the landlord may say it has been filled if he hears a southern or Spanish accent. If he says it is vacant, then when you come to look at it and he sees that you are black, Chicano, etc., he may say it has just been rented. Or, he may say he requires a security deposit equal to three month's rent, which he "forgot to put in the ad." Or he may say that the ad misprinted the rent, which is $475 not $225. Many variations on these themes can be played.*

If you suspect that the landlord is discriminating against you, it is important that you do some things to check it out. For example, if you think he is asking for a high rent or security deposit just to get rid of you, ask other tenants what they pay. The best way to check is to run a "test." Have someone who would not have trouble with discrimination (for example, a white male without kids) revisit the place soon after you do and ask if it is available and, if so, on what terms. If the response is better, the landlord was probably discriminating against you. Be sure that your friend's references, type of job and life style are similar to yours, so that the landlord cannot later say he took your friend and turned you down because of this difference.

If you need help with testing, contact one of the organizations listed at the end of this chapter, or your city's Human Relations Council.

---

*Larger landlords increasingly rely on rental agencies to take applications for them. These organizations utilize a variety of criteria to screen the prospective tenants, and are adept at choosing a legal reason (i.e., credit history) if challenged as to why one person (say a white man) got an apartment instead of another (say a black man or woman). In addition, several computerized services are offered to landlords. For a fee, they will sell landlords information about a prospective tenant's credit history, rental history, whether the tenant has ever been sued in an unlawful detainer prodeeding, etc.

IMPORTANT: A landlord can discriminate against people because they have bad credit references, are obnoxious and for other valid reasons even though they are women, disabled, from a racial minority, etc. If you are in one of the groups listed above and are turned down for a rental, it is up to you to show that the turn down was for an illegal reason (your race, sex, etc.) and not for a permissible reason (you didn't pay your rent at your last place).

B. WHAT TO DO ABOUT DISCRIMINATION

There are several different legal approaches to the problems raised by discrimination. If you are a victim of such discrimination, the next few paragraphs should be read carefully in order to decide which approach best fits your situation. Regardless of what you do, if you really want to live in the place, you must act fast, otherwise the landlord will rent it to someone else before he or she can be stopped.

1. THE DEPARTMENT OF FAIR EMPLOYMENT AND HOUSING

The State of California Department of Fair Employment and Housing takes complaints on discrimination in rental housing. This department enforces laws which prohibit housing discrimination, in addition to their other work, and has the power to order up to $1,000 damages for a tenant who has been discriminated against.

Fresno	**Sacramento**
1963 "E" Street	1201 I Street, 2nd Floor
Phone: (209) 445-5373	Phone: (916) 323-4547
Los Angeles	**San Diego**
322 West First Street, Rm. 2126	110 West C Street, Suite 1702
Phone: (213) 620-2610	Phone: (714) 237-7405
Oakland	**Santa Ana**
1111 Jackson Street	28 Civic Ctr. Plaza, Suite 330
Phone: (415) 464-4095	Phone: (714) 558-4159

San Francisco
30 Van Ness Ave.
Phone: (415) 557-2005

San Jose
888 No. First, Suite 316
Phone: (408) 277-1264

Ventura
5740 Ralston Street, Suite 104
Phone: (805) 654-4513

If you believe that you have been discriminated against, you can contact the office nearest you. You will be asked to fill out a complaint form and an investigator will be assigned to your case. You must file your complaint within 60 days of the date of the violation or of the date when you first learn of the violation. The investigator will try to work the problem out through compromise and conciliation. If this fails the Department may conduct hearings and maybe take the matter to court. It has been our experience that in recent years the Department has been slack in enforcing anti-discrimination housing laws. Therefore, after going to the Department, we would recommend that you consult a private attorney.

2. THE UNITED STATES DEPARTMENT OF HOUSING AND URBAN DEVELOPMENT (Racial, Religious & Sex Discrimination Only)

You can also lodge a complaint with the U.S. Department of Housing and Urban Development (HUD). This federal agency has most of the same powers as does the state but must let the state agency act on a case first. The HUD equal opportunity office for California is located at One Embarcadero Center in San Francisco (phone: 566-3840). HUD's power of investigation and sanctions are similar to those of the state. The experience of the authors has been that HUD is far more militant in going after discriminating landlords than is the state. However, the fact that HUD can't act until 30 days after the state has received the complaint reduces their efficiency a great deal.

3. SUE THE DISCRIMINATING LANDLORD

We think that the most effective thing you can do is to see a lawyer and sue the landlord. If you have been discriminated against because of age, sex, race, religion, physical disability or marital status, a law suit may be brought in State Court. Suits in Federal Court only work for racial or religious discrimination. If you can prove your case, you will almost certainly also be eligible to recover money damages. Many, if not most, attorneys have had little experience with discrimination law suits. This is particularly true of law suits brought in Federal Court. Rather than to try to find an attorney at random, you would be wise to check with an organization in your area dedicated to civil rights and fighting discrimination. They will undoubtedly be able to direct you to a symphathetic attorney.

Attorneys have become more interested in taking these cases in the last few years, because the amount of money that can be recovered is now substantial. For racial or religious discrimination, you can sue in federal court and collect damages to compensate you for your loss as well as substantial punitive damages and attorney's fees.* For discrimination based on age, sex, marital status, disability, having children, homosexuality, or any other "arbitrary" category, you can sue in state court and collect damages to compensate you for your loss as well as a penalty of $250 and attorney's fees.**

If you have any trouble preparing your case, need advice about whether you have been discriminated against, or just want to talk to someone about housing discrimination, volunteers will help you at your local Fair Housing Organization. For the office nearest you contact:

Southern California	Northern California
Fair Housing Council	Operation Sentinel
1525 E. 17th St., Ste. E	860 Escondido Road
Santa Ana, CA 92701	Stanford, CA 94305
(714) 835-0160	(415) 468-7464

---

*42 USC Section 3612; **Morales v. Haines**, 486 F. 2d 880 (7th Cir., 1973); **Lee v. Southern Home Sites Corp.**, 429 F. 2d 290 (5th Cir., 1970).
Federal Fair Housing Act of 1968 (42 USC §3612). For racial discrimination, you may also sue under the Civil Rights Act of 1866, which allows greater punitive damages. **Morales v. Haines, 486 F. 2d (7th Cir., 1973); **Lee v. Southern Home Sites Corp.**, 429 F. 2d 290 (5th Cir., 1970).

6
THE OBNOXIOUS LANDLORD AND YOUR RIGHT TO PRIVACY

A. YOUR RIGHTS

Some landlords can get pretty obnoxious. This is also true of plumbers, butchers, and English teachers, but since this book is for tenants we will concentrate on just the landlords. Typically, problems arise with those kinds of landlords who cannot stop fidgeting and fussing over their property. Normally, smaller landlords develop this problem to a greater extent than do the bigger, more commercial ones. Nosey landlords are always hanging around or coming by, trying to invite themselves in to look around and generally being pesty. Sometimes you may run into a manager on a power trip.

If your landlord is difficult or unpleasant to deal with, he can make your life miserable and you may not be able to do anything about it. There is no law which protects you from a disagreeable personality, and, if you have no lease, you are especially unprotected from all but the most outrageous invasions of privacy or trespass. Things can get really unpleasant, but if your right to privacy and peaceful occupancy are not disturbed, you may have

to grin and bear it or look for another place.*

Civil Code Section 1954 provides that the landlord may enter your dwelling without your consent only in the following cases:

(a) In an emergency;

(b) To make necessary or agreed repairs, decorations, alterations, or improvements, supply necessary services, or show the place to prospective or actual purchasers, mortgagers, tenants, workmen or contractors;

(c) Where the tenant has moved out;

(d) Pursuant to a court order.

Unless there is an emergency, the landlord cannot enter outside of "normal business hours" unless the tenant consents at the time of entry.

The law provides that the landlord shall not abuse his right of entry or use it to harass the tenant. The landlord must give the tenant reasonable notice of his intent to enter (24 hours is presumed to be reasonable), except in an emergency or where it is otherwise impracticable to give such notice.

Civil Code Section 1953 provides that any lease or rental agreement provision trying to waive or modify the tenant's rights under section 1954 is void.

EXAMPLE: Landlord calls tenant at nine o'clock in the morning and says he wants to show the apartment at eleven o'clock the same morning. This is inconvenient to the tenant. Can the tenant refuse to let the landlord in? Yes.

B. WHAT TO DO ABOUT IT

As you have probably figured out by now, it is one thing to have a right, and quite another thing to get the benefits of it. This is especially true for tenants. If you set about aggressively demanding

---

*Recently a court allowed a suit by a tenant alleging that a landlord was guilty of the intentional infliction of emotional distress. The court found that it was necessary to prove four things in this sort of suit: 1) outrageous conduct on the part of the landlord; 2) intention to cause or reckless disregard of the probability of causing emotional distress; 3) severe emotional suffering; and 4) actual suffering or emotional distress. **Newby v. Alto Riviera Apartments**, 131 Cal. Rptr. 547 (1976).

your rights, you may end up with a notice to vacate. Your position is slightly better if you have a lease or if you live in a rent control city, but even then the landlord will possibly take the first opportunity to find a breach in the fine print provisions and try to get rid of you. It is also generally true that you can rarely accomplish good results with hard words; never forget that the landlord holds most of the cards. This doesn't mean not to be firm or determined, but rather, not to be offensive.

If you experience any kind of problem at all during your tenancy—be it housing conditions, sanitation, disrepair, nosey landlord, etc.,—it is only common sense to begin with a polite call to your landlord about the problem. After all, he may merely be ignorant of your point of view, and may be willing to respond to a request, especially if nicely put. If, after a reasonable time, there has been no satisfactory response, put it in writing. Mention your previous oral request by the date, and ask again for prompt correction. Keep a copy for your records. If you have a manager through whom you must work, send duplicate copies to the manager and landlord.

Diplomacy varies according to the circumstances and person-alities involved. In negotiating with your landlord, it is important to always behave in a way which is most likely to convince him that in you he has as good and reliable a tenant as he can ever hope to find. This is the main strength of your position. Things will be much easier if he likes you and thinks that you can understand his problems and characteristics. It is very important for later possible action that you communicate in writing, keep copies and at all times conduct yourself reasonably.

When your best efforts have continued to the point that you consider them to have failed (how long this is depends upon how urgent or objectionable the problem is) you are faced with but a few choices: (a) you can do nothing and just live with the problem; or (b) move away; or (c) bluff (pretend you are going to get serious); or (d) stay and really fight it out.

If you choose (c) or (d), send the landlord a letter telling him "finally" that if there is not an immediate positive response you will seek legal advice, go to appropriate public authorities, or do whatever else is required to secure your rights. In making your decision of which alternative to follow, never forget that if you make the landlord angry enough, he'll make the decision for you, and you'll have to face the additional problems of a notice to vacate. At this point, it might be a good idea to see a lawyer, at least for advice and information (see Chapter 1, Part C).

One difficulty with a law suit against a landlord guilty of trespass is that it is hard to prove much in the way of money damages. Assuming you can prove the trespass occurred, the judge will probably readily agree that you have been wronged, but he may award you very little money. Most likely he will figure that you have not been harmed much by the fact that your landlord walked on your rug and opened and closed your door. However, if you can show a repeated pattern of trespass, or even one clear example of outrageous conduct, you may be able to get a substantial recovery. Unless you have a fairly good case, a law suit may cost you more than your claim is worth. However, on a limited basis you may find it financially worthwhile to hire a lawyer to contact your landlord to tell him to stop his improper conduct. You also may want to consider bringing a suit yourself in small claims court.*

NOTE: In addition to trespass, the landlord might be guilty of harassment (Code of Civil Procedure §527.6) or breach of the implied covenant of quiet enjoyment **Guntert v. Stockton**, 55 Cal. App. 3d 131 [1976]).

If your landlord comes onto your property or into your home and harms you in any way, or threatens you or damages any of your property, see an attorney. You should also report the matter to the police. Some California police departments have taken the excellent step of setting up special landlord/tenant units. The officers and legal experts in these units have been given special training in landlord/tenant law and are often helpful in compromising disputes and setting a landlord straight who has taken illegal measures against a tenant. If your city hasn't done this, why not?

Probably the time that a landlord is most likely to trespass is when the tenant has failed to pay his rent. The landlord, faced with the necessity of paying a lot of money to legally get a tenant to move out, may resort to threats or even force. While it may be

---

*See **Everybody's Guide to Small Claims Court**, Warner, Nolo Press. Order information at the back of this book.

understandable that a landlord in this situation should be mad at the tenant, this is no justification for illegal acts (we discuss illegal conduct during evictions in Chapter 11 Part A). All threats, intimidation and any physical attacks on the tenant should be reported to the police. Of course it is illegal for the landlord to come on the property and do such things as take off windows and doors, turn off the utilities or change the locks. If this is done the tenant should see an attorney at once. Do not over-react when a landlord gets hostile. While a tenant has the right to take reasonable steps to protect himself, his family and his possessions from harm, the steps must be reasonably related to the threat. The wisest thing to do whenever you fear you or your property may be harmed is to call the police.

NOTE: Here's another idea for dealing with the nosey landlord: put a small chain lock (that opens with a key) on the door. This will keep him from nosing around, but not from breaking the chain if a real emergency arises.

7
SUBSTANDARD HOUSING CONDITIONS HOW TO GET REPAIRS MADE

From time to time things are likely to go wrong with any property. Most landlords are willing to repair and maintain their places because they don't want them to get too rundown, but often you find landlords being slow and reluctant to fulfill their responsibilities. If you are having problems with your landlord in this regard, read Part A and make sure you know what your rights are, then consider all the alternatives in Part B before you decide how to start.

A. YOUR RIGHTS—THE LANDLORD'S DUTY

Under the State Housing Law and local housing codes, the landlord is required to maintain the building in a sound structural condition. This includes maintaining the roof, plumbing, and heating facilities. In addition, he is required to maintain those parts of the building and grounds which he controls (such as the stairways and halls) in a clean, sanitary and safe condition, including getting rid of insects, rodents and other pests.

The landlord's duties under the State Housing Law are spelled out in great detail in Chapter 2, part D, in the section on inspecting the premises. The requirements mentioned in that section apply not only when the landlord is trying to rent the place, but also during the time you live there.

The State Housing Law says the landlord has these duties even if he tries to impose them on you in the lease or rental agreement.

It is possible that the local government in the area in which you live will have laws which are even more strict than those enacted by the State. If you have a problem, don't hesitate to call the local Building or Health Inspector to check on this.

The landlord is also required, of course, to make any repairs he agreed to make in your lease or rental agreement.

B. GETTING REPAIRS MADE

Whenever you have a significant problem with rental property, whether it is major or minor, you should report it to your landlord.* While this may seem obvious, it apparently is not. Hopefully, once your landlord (or his authorized agent, such as the apartment manager or real estate company) has been told of your problem it will be corrected promptly. What constitutes "promptness" varies a lot with the circumstances involved. It may be reasonable for a landlord to take a week to fix a furnace in Tucson, Arizona in the summer, while it would be unreasonable for him to take two days to fix a furnace in Green Bay, Wisconsin in the winter. In deciding what is reasonable, try to be fair and to take into consideration any special problems that the landlord is having such as the inability to get a part. Try to propose sensible suggestions to your landlord if it looks as if an unavoidable delay is inevitable. For example, if the furnace breaks and it is going to take a couple of days to get it fixed, you might ask the landlord to make an empty unit available to you in the interim or to pay for a motel room for you for a few days.

If you get no response or what you believe is an inadequate response to your request that repairs be made, you should then send or give the landlord a written notice of the defects, keeping a

---

*The landlord cannot evict you if you can show that the **reason** for the attempted eviction is that you complained to him about the condition of the premises. **Kemp v. Schultz** (1981) 121 Cal.App.3d, Supp.13.

carbon or xerox copy for your records. Even though calling on the telephone is easier, you should give this notice in writing so that you have a record for later use if necessary. Your note might go something like this:

1500 Acorn Street, #4
Cloverdale, California
March 14, 19__

Smith Realty Co.
10 Jones Street
Cloverdale, California

Dear Sirs:

   I reside in apartment #4 at 1500 Acorn Street and regularly pay my rent to your office.

   On March 11, 19__ the water heater in my unit failed to function. On that date I notified your manager Mr. Robert Jackson of the problem. He called P.G.&E. on that date and they sent a man out who put a tag on the machine saying that it was no longer serviceable or safe and that is should be replaced. I gave Mr. Jackson a copy of the P.G.&E. slip on March 12, 19__ and he said that he would see about having the heater replaced immediately.

   So far the heater has not been replaced and no one has told me when it will be. I am sure you know that it is a real hardship to be without hot water. I will appreciate hearing from you as soon as possible. My telephone at work is 657-4111.

Very truly yours,

Patricia Parker

Occasionally a polite but firm approach does not work. In that case, you are simply faced with the fact that the landlord is not going to make needed repairs voluntarily. There are legal steps that a tenant can take to get major defects repaired, but before deciding anything you should sit down with yourself and figure out what you are getting into.

If you need to get repairs made you have several approaches available to you:

1. Withhold your rent payments.
2. Get help from the local authorities.
3. Pay for repairs out of your rent.
4. Sue the landlord.
5. Stay and forget the whole thing.
6. Move out.

Read the discussion below on each one of them before deciding what to do. Keep it in mind that any method you use to pressure and force your landlord into making repairs can possibly escalate into a long and troublesome conflict. The landlord is almost certain to get alienated on a personal level, and he may start looking for the first excuse to get rid of you for being a troublesome tenant. There are protections against retaliation, which we discuss below, but they have definite limits. On the other hand, you have the right to live in safe, decent housing and your landlord has the duty to provide it. Ultimately, what you decide to do depends upon all the facts and personalities in your own particular case. After reading the sections below, if you are still uncertain or unclear, then you should consider getting advice from a tenants' rights project or an attorney (see Chapter 1, Part C).

1. RENT WITHHOLDING

Because of a decision of the California Supreme Court in the famous **Green v. Superior Court** case, California tenants have a powerful weapon to use in their battles to get substandard housing improved.* Previously, tenants had been relatively weak in this area, but now the tables are turning.

Under the rules of this new court decision, whenever the landlord fails to comply with housing codes by refusing to make proper repairs, the tenant now has the right to withhold rent payments (and, eventually, he may even get to keep part of it) **if** the circumstances are right and if he properly asserts his rights.**

All leases and rental agreements are now deemed by the law to include an "implied warranty of habitability." This means that whether it is actually written down or not, and whether he likes it or not, the landlord is required as a condition of any rental agreement to maintain the place in a habitable condition, as defined by the Housing Code.

If your landlord violates ("breaches") his obligation to you under this warranty, you may have the right to withhold rent payments **if** his breach was "material." What is a "material" breach has yet to be clearly defined by the law, but here are some guidelines the court has set out. Both the seriousness of the defect and the length of time it persists are relevant factors in deciding if it was material. Minor code violations will not be considered material. Nor will violations which do not affect the tenant's apartment or the common areas he uses. Thus, failure to correct heavy rat infestation for a month would be clearly material, while a few ants which came in on one occasion when it rained would not. No heat for a week in January might be material, while a doorway an inch lower than allowed by the codes would not. Until the rules on this issue are more fully developed, you will just have to use common sense as to what is "material."***

---

*Green v. Superior Court, 10 Cal 3d 616 (1974). Many of these issues raised by Green are discussed in Moskovitz, **The Implied Warranty of Habitability—A New Doctrine Raising New Issues**, 62 California Law Review 1444 (1974).

This is true even if the defects were present **when the tenant moved in. Knight v. Halstrammer (1981) 171 Cal.Rptr. 707.

***Courts have generally found that the conditions set out as untenantable in section 1941.1 also apply here.

If the breach is material, you may exercise your right to withhold rent only if (a) the defect was not caused by you, anyone living with you or a guest or visitor of yours, and (b) the landlord has notice of the defects. You are not legally required to give written notice—an oral demand will do, but it won't be as easy to prove later on. You can use the form "Notice to Repair" set out below to give the landlord written notice.

If the landlord fails after notice to properly make the repairs, do not make your next rent payment. Although not required by law, it may be a good idea to give the landlord a second note at this time telling him what you are doing. It might look like the notice on the following page.

If the landlord then makes the repairs, you must resume your regular rent payments the next month, but you do **not** have to pay him the full amount of the rent you already withheld. You only owe him a "reasonable rent" out of that. What is a "reasonable rent" depends on the circumstances and has **not** yet been clearly defined by the law. In one New Jersey case where the landlord had failed to provide heat, hot water, elevator service and incinerator use, the court required the tenant to pay as much as 75% of the agreed rent.*   A West Virginia case allows the "reasonable rent" to be measured by determining the tenant's damages for "discomfort and annoyance" and then subtracting this amount from the agreed rent** It is not clear whether California courts will allow this, however.*** If you and your landlord can't agree on this, you could keep the money and let him take you to court if he wants to. On the other hand, it may not be worth the trouble. If you do keep the extra money, and if he does go to court, and if you prove that he materially breached his "implied warranty of habitability" and you give him notice to repair and he failed to do so in a reasonable time, the court will decide what is a reasonable rent and make you pay only that amount.

If you follow the procedures in this section, then when you refuse to pay your rent, it is quite likely that the landlord will give you a "three-day notice" to pay your rent in three days or get out.

---

*Academy Spires, Inc. v. Brown, 111 N.J. Spr. 477, 268 A. 2d 556, 562 (1970). In a recent California case rent was reduced by 50%, Strickland v. Becks, 95 CA 3d Supp 18 (1979).

**Teller v. McCoy, 253 S.E. 2d 114, 128 (W. Va Supreme Ct., 1978).

***Quevado v. Braga, 72 Cal. App. Supp. 3d 1 (1977). But see Stoiber v. Honeychuck (1980) 101 Cal. App. 3d 903.

Then, when you fail to do either, he'll sue to have you evicted (see Chapter 12 for a full discussion of the eviction procedure). While normally he would easily win such a suit, in this case you have a good defense, and he will not be allowed to evict you if you can prove that he materially breached his implied warranty of habitability.

When you raise this defense in your case, the judge may then order you to make future rent payments into court until the law suit is concluded. (He may **not** order you to pay into court the rent you already withheld.)

At the end of the trial, if you have proved your case, the court will decide what was a "reasonable rent" while the defects on the premises were not corrected. When this is decided, that portion of the rent money which you paid into court which represents "reasonable rent" will be paid to the landlord, and the balance will be returned to you. Also, the landlord will receive a judgment for the reasonable rent portion of the rent you withheld. He will .**not** get an eviction order, and he should not recover his attorney's fees or court costs either, since you really won the case (in fact, **you** should be able to get **your** attorney's fees and court costs).

If you do not have a lease, the landlord might try to get you out simply by giving you a 30-day notice to vacate (rather than a three-day notice to pay the rent or get out). If you refuse to move and can prove in the eviction law suit he brings that he gave you the notice to retaliate against you for rightfully withholding your rent, then this might well be held to be an attempted illegal "retaliation eviction" and you will not be evicted. Actually, the California courts have not yet dealt with retaliation in this type of situation, but a case from the District of Columbia held this kind of retaliation to be illegal. **Robinson v. Diamond Housing Corp.**, 463 F.2d 853 (D.C. Cir. 1972). A California statute seems to protect against retaliation in such a situation since it forbids a landlord from retaliating against a tenant's lawful exercise of his rights. Civil Code Section 1942.5(c).*

Rent withholding is a powerful strategy. If all goes according to the law stated above you can stay in the premises, withhold rent and win eviction actions until the premises are brought up to code. Unfortunately, you might get into a law suit and require an attorney's services. Quite often, however, the written threat of rent withholding is sufficient to solve the problem.

NOTE: On occasion, a tenant has claimed in court that he or she had a valid reason for withholding rent because of substandard conditions, when in fact the unit was clearly habitable. These tenants were simply trying to get out of paying rent. This has resulted in **some** judges being cynical about all cases where tenants have withheld rent under the theory that the landlord has breached the duty to provide a habitable dwelling. When you add this fact to another one—judges are more likely to be landlords than tenants—you can see that a tenant is sometimes at a disadvantage in a rent withholding case. We don't mean to scare you so much that you will not use the rent withholding remedy, but we do want to prepare you for what you may face. How can you counter this possible disadvantage in a rent withholding case? Make sure to tell the judge clearly that you have the money to pay the rent, have always paid rent in the past, and will immediately start paying rent as soon as the proper repairs are made. Also, be sure that you have strong documentation that the uninhabitable condition really exists.

If you withhold rent and the landlord sues to evict, and you fail to convince the court that the landlord breached the implied

---

*In **Barela v. Superior Court** (1981) 178 Cal.Rptr. 618, the California Supreme Court held that an eviction based on a tenant's criminal complaint against the landlord was retaliatory and prohibited both under Civil Code Section 1942.5 and common law (law made by courts).

warranty of habitability, you may be evicted for nonpayment of rent. Therefore, rather than withholding rent—an alternative strategy is to pay the rent and sue the landlord in small claims court because he failed to make repairs. This remedy also carries some risk of subsequent eviction notice, but this should be easier to defend against, under the rule which forbids "retaliatory" evictions.*

NOTICE OF RENT WITHHOLDING

To_____, Landlord of the premises located at _____

NOTICE IS HEREBY GIVEN that because of your failure to comply with your implied warranty of habitability by refusing to repair (list defects) on the premises, as previously demanded of you on date(s) within a reasonable time after such demand, the undersigned tenant has elected to withhold this month's rent in accordance with California law. Rent payments will be resumed in the future, as they become due, only after said defects have been properly repaired.

Dated: _____

_____
(Signature of tenant)

Authority: **Green v. Superior Court**, 10 Cal 3d 616
            (Jan 15., 1974).

(This form should be used after there has been no response to the "Notice to Repair" form.

---

*See Civil Code Sec. 1942.5(c).

2. GO TO THE LOCAL AUTHORITIES

The State Housing Law and local housing codes are supposed to be enforced by a city or county agency. Codes are usually enforced by an agency called the Building Inspection or Housing Department (or some similar name). Violations creating immediate health hazards (such as rats or broken toilets) are also enforced by the Health Department. Violations creating fire hazards (such as trash in the basement) are also enforced by the Fire Department. Effective January 1983, state law has been further tightened to provide jail terms of up to one year for repeated severe violations of the state housing law and fines up to $5,000. Health & Safety Code 17995.3.

These agencies have the power to close the building and even demolish it if the landlord will not comply with their orders to correct code violations. They very seldom go to this extreme, however. Usually they inspect the building, send a letter to the landlord ordering him to make repairs, and later reinspect the building and send more letters until the landlord complies.*

This sort of pressure works on many landlords, so your reporting code violations to the agency and asking for an inspection can sometimes help you. If you decide to do this, it is best to go to the agency and make your complaint in writing.

There are, however, some things to watch out for before deciding to report code violations.

First, if the place is **really** bad, constituting a real health or fire hazard which the landlord will be unable to remedy soon, the agency just might close the building down, kicking you out in the process. This doesn't help you, unless you just want to get back at the landlord. If you are afraid this might happen, see if you can find out the name of someone in the agency who is friendly to tenants. Call this person and see what the agency is likely to do.

Second, if the landlord owns a lot of slum property or has been in this business for a while, he probably knows what to do to keep the agency off his back.** He may be friendly with the building

---

*Another remedy was set up in 1974. If the landlord has failed for six months or more to comply with agency orders to repair, the enforcement agency is required to notify the state's Franchise Tax Board (enforcement agencies have the discretion to in 90 days). The Board then denies the landlord any deduction on his state income tax form for interest, taxes, or depreciation on the building. California Revenue & Taxation Code Sections 17299 and 24436.5.

**Enforcement is particularly poor in our older, larger cities such as San Francisco, Oakland, and Los Angeles.

inspectors. He may know how to take appeals which can delay enforcement of the codes for years. He may make a few repairs and let the others go, knowing just how much it takes to temporarily satisfy the agency that he is "trying." The landlord is less likely to get away with these tricks if there is a real health or fire hazard, like rats or open gasoline on the premises. The Health or Fire Departments will usually be tougher than the Building Inspection Department.

Third, there is a danger that the landlord will find out that you reported him to the agency and will try to evict you because of this. This is called a "retaliatory eviction." The landlord will usually do this simply by giving you a 30-day notice terminating your month-to-month tenancy, giving no reason for his doing so. Or, he might give you a 30-day notice that your rent is being increased as an indirect way of getting you out.

Retaliatory evictions for reporting code violations are illegal for 180 days after the date the report was made. So, if you refuse to get out and the landlord sues to evict you and you prove he is doing it because you reported the code violation, you will win the lawsuit. The problem is that **you** have the burden of proof. If the landlord can show that he is evicting you for some good reason (for example, you violated the rental agreement), you might lose. However, by attempting a retaliatory eviction, the landlord is taking a chance too. If you get out because of his 30-day notice but can prove it was retaliatory, you can sue him for money damages later.*

If you have a lease, you are pretty well protected from retaliatory evictions, since the landlord must prove a good reason to kick you out before your lease is up. If you have only a month-to-month rental agreement, you do face the danger of retaliatory evictions, **unless** you have a provision like Paragraph 16 of the Model Month-to-Month Rental Agreement inside the back cover of this book. That paragraph requires the landlord to state his reasons when trying to terminate your tenancy or increase the rent, and to prove these reasons are true if you question them. Also, tenants in certain rent control cities can only be evicted for "good cause" as specified in the law (see Chapter 15).

---

*__Aweeka v. Bonds__, 20 Cal. App 3d 278 (1971).

When deciding whether to withhold rent, sue the landlord or take other action against him, you may wish to find out if he has had trouble with the housing code inspection before. In the past, many code inspectors have refused to show tenants their records without the landlord's permission. A new statute, however, expressly decares that all records of notices and orders directed to the landlord concerning serious code violations (those listed in Civil Code §1941.1), and the inspector's acts regarding those violations are **public records**. Government Code §6254.7(c). Every citizen has the right to inspect any public record. Government Code §6253.

3. REPAIR IT YOURSELF

Where your landlord refuses to make repairs, California law gives you the right to make the repairs yourself (or hire someone to do them) and deduct the cost from your next month's rent. There are, however, some restrictions on this right, and there are certain procedures you must follow to exercise this right. The law on this subject is stated in California Civil Code Sections 1941-1942.5. Before you decide to use the repair and deduct remedy, re-read the previous pages—rent withholding is often a far easier and more effective remedy.

a. Restrictions on the Right to Repair and Deduct

First, this remedy can be used only for certain defects. It can be used only if your place substantially lacks any of the following (C.C. 1941.1):

- effective waterproofing and weather protection of roof and exterior walls, including unbroken windows and doors;
- plumbing and gas facilities maintained in good working order;
- a water system which produces hot and cold running water;
- heating facilities maintained in good working order;
- lighting and wiring maintained in good working order;
- building and grounds clean of trash, rodents and vermin;
- an adequate number of garbage cans and trash barrels, kept in clean condition and good repair;
- floors, stairways and railings maintained in good repair.

Second, you are not allowed to use this remedy if you interfered with the landlord's attempt to repair the defect, or if the defect was caused by your violation of any of the following duties, under Civil Code Section 1941.2:

- to keep your premises clean (unless the landlord has agreed to do this);
- to properly dispose of your garbage and trash (unless the landlord has agreed to do this);
- to properly use all electrical, gas and plumbing fixtures and keep them as clean as their condition permits;
- not to permit any person on the premises with your permission to willfully damage the premises or the facilities, or to do so yourself;
- to use each room only for the purpose for which it was intended (for example, you can't sleep in the dining room).

Finally, you cannot use your "repair-and-deduct" remedy more than twice in any 12 month period.

b. How to Exercise Your Right to Repair and Deduct

If you come within the above restrictions, you can use your repair and deduct remedy.

To do so, you must first notify the landlord of the defects he should repair. You should put this in writing, date it and keep a copy so you can later prove you did it. Below is a form notice you might use. Be sure to keep a **copy** of this notice to use if you later go to court.

Next you must wait a "reasonable time" to give the landlord a chance to make the repairs. After a reasonable time runs out, you can do the repairs. What is a "reasonable time" will depend on the circumstances. If the heat doesn't work in January, a reasonable wait may mean only a few days, at most. If it breaks down in June, and it is expensive to repair quickly, you should wait a little longer. If you have complained to the landlord about the defect before, then you should not have to wait too long. The law says that 30 days is "presumed" to be a reasonable time. This means that if you do not wait 30 days, if the case goes to court, **you** must prove the wait was reasonable. If you wait 30 days, the landlord must prove the wait was unreasonable.

NOTICE TO REPAIR

To _____ , Landlord of the premises
located at _____ .

NOTICE IS HEREBY GIVEN that unless certain defects on
the premises are repaired within a reasonable time, the
undersigned tenant shall exercise any and all rights accru-
ing to him pursuant to law, including those granted by
California Civil Code Sections 1941–42 and **Green v.
Superior Court.**

The defects are the following:

_____
_____
_____

Dated: _____

_____
(signature of tenant)

If the landlord has not made the repairs after a reasonable time,
you may do the repairs or hire someone to do them. Keep a record
of all the time you put in and all amounts you spend on labor and
materials.

When the next month's rent is due, give the landlord a written
statement itemizing the expenses of the repairs, including compensation for your time. If this adds up to less than the rent, you
must pay him the balance.

REMEMBER: You cannot use your repair and deduct remedy in
more than two months in any one year and cannot deduct more
than one month's rent at a time.

c. Retaliation for using Repair and Deduct Remedy

If you have a month-to-month rental agreement instead of a
lease, the landlord might try to retaliate against you by giving you a

30-day notice terminating your tenancy or raising your rent.* The problems this raises are discussed above. In addition, there are some special restrictions on the tenant's right to stop retaliations against using the repair and deduct remedy (C.C. 1942.5):

- The tenant is protected only for 180 days after he gives the notice of the defects. After that, the landlord can terminate the tenancy or raise the rent, even if the tenant can prove that the landlord is doing it to retaliate.
- The tenant can raise the defense of retaliatory eviction in an eviction law suit only if he is paid up in his rent when he raises the defense.
- The tenant can raise the defense in an eviction lawsuit only if he has not raised this defense in another eviction action brought by the same landlord in the past 12 months.

NOTE: The restrictions that apply to the repair and deduct remedy don't apply to rent withholding (see above).

4. SUE THE LANDLORD

Where the landlord has failed to make repairs which result in a breach of the implied warranty of habitability (discussed in Section B1 of this chapter) and you haven't withheld your rent, you may sue your landlord to get back some (or even all) of the rent you paid while the landlord was in breach of the warranty.** In some situations this will be less than $1500 and, if this is the case, you should consider bringing your suit in Small Claims Court. **Everybody's Guide to Small Claims Court**, Warner, Nolo Press, is an excellent guide as to how to use this court.***

---

*He cannot do this if he has agreed to the Model Month-by-Month Rental Agreement discussed in Chapter 2, Part B of the Handbook, because of paragraph 16, or if you live in a rent control area where "good cause" is required for evictions. See Chapter 15.

Quevado v. Braga, 72 Cal. App. 3d Supp. 1 (1977). **Stoiber v. Honeychuck, 162 Cal Rptr 194 (1980). The **Stoiber** case is a very strong one which recognizes the possibility that a tenant might be able to recover punitive damages if the landlord's conduct is willful and that a tenant may also be able to recover on a theory of intentional infliction of emotional distress. A model complaint to use when suing a landlord for breach of the implied warranty of habitability appears on the Forms section of the latest supplement to the California Eviction Defense Manual (CEB, 1970).

***If the conditions in your place were horrible and/or you suffered true emotional distress, the amount of money recoverable under **Stoiber v. Honeychuck** and other court decisions may be in excess of the $1500 small claims maximum. This is an area where you might want to consult a lawyer (see Chapter 1, Section C).

5. MOVE OUT

As a last resort, you might simply move out. Under the law, if the landlord's failure to do his duty substantially interferes with your ability to use and enjoy the premises, you can move out in the middle of your lease or rental agreement, without first notifying him that you are doing so. What is "substantial interference" depends on the circumstances. A few ants which come in when it rains might not be, but constant rat infestation would be. You will not be held responsible for any further rent.

This is called the doctrine of "constructive eviction." After you move out, you can also sue the landlord for money damages. You'll need to see a lawyer about pursuing such a suit (see Chapter 1, Part C).

If you decide to move out, send the landlord a written notice, such as the one below, and keep a copy for your files.

1500 Acorn Street, #4
Cloverdale, California
March 19, 19___

Smith Realty Co.
10 Jones Street
Cloverdale, California

Dear Sirs:

I reside in apartment #4 at 1500 Acorn Street and regularly pay rent to your office.

As you know, on March 11, 19___ the water heater in my unit broke down. Although I have repeatedly requested repairs, no action has yet been taken. Because of the weather and because of the size of my family, I cannot continue to live comfortably without such an essential service, so I am therefore compelled to exercise my rights under Civil Code Section 1942 to vacate the premises.

If repairs are not made by March 24, 19___ I will vacate the premises and seek whatever other remedies I am entitled to under law.

Very truly yours,

Patricia Parker

8
INJURIES
TO A TENANT
DUE TO SUBSTANDARD
HOUSING CONDITIONS

When we start talking about personal injuries, we get into an area that lawyers call "Torts." Whole books have been written on this subject and many lawyers make a nice living filing lawsuits on behalf of people who have been injured as a result of the "negligent" or "intentional" acts of others. While we don't deal with this subject in detail, the last several years have seen a great increase in the ways a landlord might be held responsible for injuries caused to a tenant. Landlords may be liable for physical injuries caused by faulty premises (a broken stair, for example) and for mental suffering or emotional distress caused by slum conditions, wrongful evictions, invasions of privacy and harassment. A tenant may even recover against the landlord for maintaining a nuisance if the premises are substantially below code or abnormally messy or loud tenants are allowed to remain in other units in the building. If you are injured, either physically or mentally as a result of some act or failure to act of your landlord, you should see a lawyer. (If your injury is worth $1500 or less to you, you may want to go to Small Claims Court.)

It used to be that a landlord could put a clause in a lease or rental agreement which freed him of most responsibility for injuries suffered by a tenant, even if the injury was a direct result of the landlord's negligence. This is no longer the law,* although you will still find this sort of unenforceable clause in some leases and rental agreements. Today a landlord is held to the same duty of care toward his tenants as our society imposes on everyone else in their dealings with each other. Basically, the rule is that a landlord must act toward his tenant as a reasonable person would, considering all the circumstances. If a landlord acts in an unreasonable way and an injury occurs, he or she can be held financially responsible.**

A. HERE ARE SOME EXAMPLES OF SITUATIONS WHERE COURTS HAVE HELD THAT LANDLORDS COULD BE LIABLE FOR A TENANT'S INJURIES: ***

- Mental distress from slum conditions. **Stoiber v. Honeychuck**, 162 Cal.Rptr. 194 (1980).
- Fall through a handrail on stairway. **Brennan v. Cockrell**, 35 C.A. 3d. 796 (1973).
- Fire as a result of defective heater. **Golden v. Conway**, 55 C.A. 3d. 948. This case also states that a landlord can be strictly liable (the tenant doesn't have to prove that the landlord acted in an unreasonable way) if he installs an appliance without knowing whether or not it is defective.
- Fire as a result of defective wiring. **Evans v. Thompson**, 72 C.A. 3d. 978 (1977). Here a defective wall plug that the tenant had asked the landlord to fix forced the tenant to plug a refrigerator into another socket with an extension cord which resulted in a fire.
- Rape as a result of lax security. **O'Hara v. Western Seven Trees Corp.**, 75 Cal. App. 3d. (1977). Landlord could be liable where security was inadequate and landlord knew of danger of rape and didn't tell tenant.
- Tenant trips over rock on common stairway. **Henrioulle v.**

---

*California Civil Code Section 1953.

Brennan v. Cockrell, 35 C.A. 3d. 796 (1973), California Civil Code Section 1714.

***A California Court of Appeal recently ruled that a landlord is strictly liable for injuries to a tenant caused by a defect in the rental property, even if the landlord neither caused the defect nor knew about it. **Becker v. IRM Corp.**, 144 C.A. 3d 321 (1983). The case is presently pending on appeal to the California Supreme Court; it should not be relied on until the court renders its decision.

Marin Ventures, Inc., 20 Cal. 3d. 512 (1978).
- Emotional distress at intimidation by landlord in course of eviction. **Newby v. Alto Riviera Apts**, 131 Cal.Rptr. 547 (1976).

This list is not meant to be exhaustive, just to give you some idea of the state of the law.*

B. HERE ARE SOME EXAMPLES WHERE LANDLORDS HAVE AND HAVE NOT BEEN HELD TO BE RESPONSIBLE FOR THE INJURIES OF NON-TENANTS (VISITORS)

- Vicious dog bites visitor. **Ucello v. Landenslayer**, 44 C.A. 3d. 504 (1975). Landlord was held liable when a tenant's dog bit a visitor when landlord knew that the dog was vicious and did nothing about it.
- Injury in gunfight. **Totten v. More Oakland**, 63 C.A. 3d 538 (1976). A minor (the guest of a tenant) was injured in a gunfight in the laundry room of an apartment building. The court held that, as no similar episode had occurred before, the landlord was not liable.
- Landlord has no duty to protect tenant from the unforeseen acts of intruders where there is no history of violence in the area. **Riley v. Marcus**, 177 Cal.Rptr. 827.

NOTE ON HIRING AN ATTORNEY: We discuss lawyers in Chapter 1. You will want to read this chapter, but you should also realize that personal injury cases are special in that a lawyer normally does not charge the client any money up front, but takes a portion of any recovery. This is called a contingency fee and means that the lawyer gets nothing if you lose. Depending on how much work is involved, the fee can be from 25% to 50% of the recovery. It is wise to shop around to see what various lawyers offer. If you have a strong case, you should get someone to help you for 25% of the eventual recovery.

Here is another idea that might prove helpful. Contact the landlord or his insurance company yourself and see what they will offer you without an attorney. Then, if you think you should get

---

*Other California cases are discussed in an article at 12 San Diego Law Review 401 (1975).

more, hire an attorney on a contingency fee arrangement so that he or she only gets a cut of the amount they can recover for you **over and above** what you were offered without their help.

new!

nolo software!

Will Writer

by Legisoft $39.95

You answer basic questions about marital status, children, your residency, property you own, etc. The WILLWRITER program then directs you to make choices about what you would like done with your property. Your will is printed with instructions for execution and storage. A manual provides lots of helps in areas such as tax planning and probate avoidance. Runs on Apple II+, IIc, IIe and the IBM PC (and most PC compatibles). Valid in all the United States (except Louisiana).

"Fortunately, the manual is well worth reading. Like the Nolo books, it provides concise, practical information in terms any reasonably intelligent person can understand. It uses legal buzzwords only when necessary, and it includes a glossary to help you keep the terminology straight."

A + Magazine, November 1984

"Several days ago somebody handed me a little packet of information which included a floppy disk and I can't resist, everytime I see a floppy disk I have to stick it in a computer somewhere and see what's on it. I usually find out, this is a rule of thumb now, that a lot of software promises more than it delivers and the company charges you more than they should. This is not the case with WillWriter. I took a copy of WillWriter home, punched it up, went thru the questions, filled out the answers, and the thing printed out about a four page will—right in front of my eyes." . . . Jim Eason, KGO Radio

Qty	Title	Price	Total
	WillWriter	$39.95	

Name _____

Address _____

_____

VISA—

MC —   Tax (CA) _____

Subtotal _____

_____   UPS $2.00

Exp. date _____   Total _____

Signature _____

Send to: Nolo Press
          950 Parker St.
          Berkeley, CA 94710
          (415) 549-1976

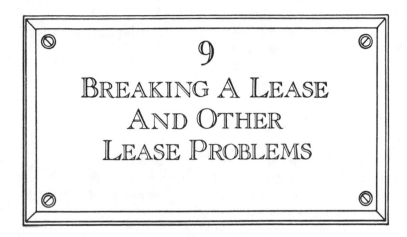

9
BREAKING A LEASE
AND OTHER
LEASE PROBLEMS

A. WHAT HAPPENS WHEN
THE LEASE RUNS OUT

Often a tenant wishes to stay in a dwelling after a lease term expires. If you are in this situation, read your lease carefully as it may have a provision covering this situation. If so, the terms of the lease control unless they call for an illegal automatic renewal. In the absence of a lease provision, California Civil Code section 1945 provides that if a lease runs out and the landlord thereafter accepts rent, the tenant becomes a month-to-month tenant under the same terms as are in the old lease. All the terms of the original lease, with the exception of the period of occupancy clause, are still binding and become what is, in effect, a written rental agreement (see Chapter 2, Part B). This means that either the landlord or the tenant can terminate the tenancy with a 30-day written notice, likewise, the rent can be increased after a 30-day notice.*

Sometimes a lease will contain a provision calling for the automatic renewal of the lease if the tenant stays beyond the end of the

---

*Special rules on the termination of a tenancy are in effect in some cities which have rent control ordinances. See Chapter 15.

lease term. This would mean that if a tenant held over one day after a one year lease expired, he would have renewed the lease for another year. This sort of provision is legal only if the renewal or extension provision is printed in at least eight point boldface type immediately above the place where the tenant signs the lease. If a renewal provision is not set forth in this way it is voidable by the tenant (C.C. 1942.5).

B. HOW TO SUBLEASE

A sublease is what happens when you lease or rent your place to someone else, and you move out and they move in. The subtenant pays an agreed-upon rent to you (it can be more or less than the amount you pay) and you pay rent to the landlord. Sometimes it is possible to have the subtenant pay directly to the landlord. When you sublease you become, in a real sense, a landlord, and must start thinking like one, at least in regard to collecting rent and protecting the condition of the premises. When you sublease, you are still responsible for all of the terms and conditions of your own lease to the landlord. This means that if your subtenant doesn't pay up or if he wrecks the place, you will be liable to the landlord.

Technically speaking, you are only entitled to sublease when you have a lease yourself in the first place. However, most leases require the landlord's consent and it used to be accepted that the landlord could withhold his consent arbitrarily. There is some recent case law that indicates that a landlord cannot unreasonably withhold consent.* In addition, the lease can't be made for a period that extends beyond the end of the original lease. If you have a lease for one year and only seven months remain under it, then, technically, the longest time you can sublease the place is seven months.

As a matter of practice, subleases are often made for periods of time in excess of the original lease. Often, in fact, people with no lease at all will "sublease" their place for a few months while they are on vacation, or the like. This is not, technically speaking, a valid

---

*Civil Code Section 1945.5, **In re Cox** (1970) 3 Cal. 3d 205, 55 Calif. State Bar Journal 108 (1980).

sublease,and while it may work in practice, if something goes wrong, you may find yourself over a barrel.

Whenever you let anyone move into your place for a while, it is important to have a written agreement which sets out all the terms of the arrangement. We include here an example of a possible sublease arrangement with the warning that it will have to be modified to suit your individual circumstances.

SUBLEASE AGREEMENT

This is an agreement between Patricia Parker of 1500 Acorn Street #4, Cloverdale California and Joan Ehrman now residing at 77 Wheat Avenue, Berkeley, California.

1. In consideration of $200 per motnh payable on the first day of each month Patricia Parker agrees to sublease apartment #4 at 1500 Acorn Street, Cloverdale, California to Joan Ehrman from August 1, 19__ to December 30, 19__.

2. Patricia Parker hereby acknowledges receipt of $500 which represents payment of the first and last months' rent and a $100 cleaning and damage deposit.* The $100 cleaning and damage deposit will be returned to Joan Ehrman on December 30, 19__ if the premises are completely clean and have suffered no damage.

3. A copy of the agreement between Smith Realty and Patricia Parker is stapled to this agreement and is incorporated as if set out in full. Joan Ehrman specifically covenants and agrees to adhere to all the rules and regulations set out in sections 1-10 of this lease.

_____   _____
Date   Patricia Parker

_____   _____
Date   Joan Ehrman

---

*The rules which limit the amount of money that a landlord can charge a tenant for deposits also apply to sub-lease agreements.

C. HOW TO BREAK A LEASE

1. GENERAL RULES

Often a tenant wants to move before the lease runs out. This need not be a great problem. The same shortage of housing that gives the landlord an advantage at the time of the original rental also makes it possible for a tenant to get out of a lease fairly easily. When you sign a lease you sign a contract by which you promise to pay rent on certain premises for a certain time (see Chapter 2, Part B). Simply moving out does not get you off the hook as far as paying is concerned. You have made a contract and legally you are bound to fulfill it. This means that you are legally bound to pay rent for the full lease term whether or not you continue to occupy the dwelling.* If you do not pay, your landlord can sue you, get a judgment and try to collect the money by doing such things as attaching your wages, either now or in the future.

Indeed, the picture for a tenant breaking a lease would be very bleak were it not for the legal doctrine of contract law that the landlord must take all reasonable steps to keep his damages to a minimum. This means that when the tenant leaves in the middle of the lease term, the landlord must make all reasonable efforts to rent the premises to another tenant at the best price possible. The amount of money, if any, that the landlord can recover from the original tenant is the difference between what the tenant was obligated to pay the landlord under the terms of the lease and what the landlord can get by leasing the premises to someone else for the same period of time. Because of a general shortage of rental units in most areas of California the landlord should be able to get a new tenant fairly quickly for about the same rental as paid by the original tenant. The result is that the tenant who breaks the lease is obligated for little or no damages.**

2. SELF-PROTECTION WHEN BREAKING A LEASE

Notify your landlord in writing as soon as you know that you are going to move before the end of a lease term. The more notice you

---

*Civil Code section 1951.2.
**WARNING! If your lease contains a clause that says you have the right to sublease or assign (transfer) the lease, either with or without the landlord's permission, you must be careful. Civil Code section 1951.4 requires that you find a suitable tenant to take your place in this situation. If you fail to do this, your landlord may be able to sit on his hands and let your rent pile up with no duty to re-rent the place himself (mitigate damages). The law is confused in this area, but to be on the safe side you should find a new tenant, or if the landlord is being difficult, tenants, to take your place.

give the landlord the better your chances are that he will find another tenant. Send a letter like the one set out here.

1500 Acorn Street #4
Cloverdale, California
September 15, 19___

Smith Realty Co.
10 Jones Street
Cloverdale, California

Dear Sirs:

As you know, I occupy unit #4 of your building at 1500 Acorn Street under a lease that runs from June 1, 19___ until May 31, 19___.

Due to circumstances beyond my control it is necessary for me to move on October 31, 19___. As I paid my last month's rent when I moved in I will make no rent payment on October 1, 19___ and will ask that you apply my last month's rent to the month of October.

I apologize for any inconvenience you may have by my moving out before the end of my lease term and will cooperate with you in every way to see that a new tenant is found promptly. Of course, I will rely on you to mitigate any damages as much as possible.

Yours truly,

Patricia Parker

REMINDER: When you send this notice you have in theory violated your lease contract. Your landlord could try to evict you using a three-day notice (see Chapter 11). This is very unlikely, however, as you will have moved out before the matter gets into court.

After sending the landlord your written notice it is wise to stop by and talk to him. He may have another tenant ready to move in and not be concerned by your moving out. In some cases the landlord may demand an amount of money to compensate him for his trouble in re-renting the place. If the amount is small it may be easier to agree to pay rather than to become involved in a dispute. If your landlord has a security and/or cleaning deposit, you might offer to let him keep all or part of these in full settlement of all possible damage claims arising from your leaving in the middle of the lease term. As noted above, since the landlord has a duty to try and re-rent the place ("mitigate damages") and since this is reasonably easy to do, you should not agree to pay much in the way of damages. Get any agreement you make in writing.

If it is not possible to deal rationally with your landlord, or if he won't make a written release, you should take steps to protect yourself. Don't let your landlord scare you into paying him a lot of money. Simply put an advertisement in your local paper to lease your dwelling at the same rental that you are paying. When people call, show them the place, but tell them that any lease arrangement must be worked out with your landlord. Give the names of all interested parties to your landlord. Also request that the potential tenants contact the landlord directly. To protect yourself keep a list of all tenants who appear suitable and who express an interest in moving in. Include information on your list that indicates the potential tenants are "responsible," such as job and family. Write a letter to your landlord with a list of the names and keep a copy for your file. He has a right to approve or disapprove of whomever you suggest as a tenant, but he may not be unreasonable about it.

AGREEMENT

This agreement is between Patricia Parker of 1500 Acorn Street #4, Cloverdale, California, and Smith Realty Co., of 10 Jones Street, Cloverdale, California, and by its owner, B. R. Smith.

In consideration of the amount of $75, Smith Realty Co. hereby agrees to cancel the lease of Patricia Parker on Apt. #4 at 1500 Acorn Street, Cloverdale, California as of October 31, 19____. The $75 payment is hereby acknowledged to be made this date by cancelling the obligation of Smith Realty Co. to return to Patricia Parker the $75 security deposit paid on June 1, 19____.

Date   B. R. Smith

Date   Patricia Parker

1500 Acorn Street #4
Cloverdale, California
October 1, 19___

Smith Realty Co.
10 Jones Street
Cloverdale, California

Dear Sirs:

As I told you on September 15, 19___, I plan to move out of this apartment on October 31, 19___. Because I wish to keep damages to a minimum I am herewith including the names, addresses, and phone numbers of four people who have expressed an interest in renting this apartment on or about November 1, 19___ at the same rent that I pay. I assume that you will find one of these potential tenants to be suitable, unless of course you have already arranged to rent the apartment.

(include list of names and addresses)

Very truly yours,

Patricia Parker

3. POSSIBLE LEGAL ACTION

After a tenant moves out and breaks a lease he can be sued. This is not likely if the landlord has gotten a new tenant to move in almost immediately after the old tenant moves out, because in such a situation there would be little or no damages. However, occasionally it will take the landlord a little time or expense such as advertising to get a new tenant. In this case he may sue either in Small Claims Court or possibly in Municipal Court.

If you are sued you will have to read the complaint carefully to see if the amount the landlord asks for is fair. As explained above if you take the proper steps to protect yourself he should be entitled to little or nothing. In unusual situations, however, the landlord may be entitled to some recovery. An example of one situation where damages could be recovered would be where a tenant with a year's lease at a $400 per month rental moved out in mid-year and no new tenant could be found who would pay more than $375 per month. In this case the old tenant would be liable for the $25 a month difference between what he paid and what the new tenant paid, multiplied by the number of months left in the lease at the time he moved out. A tenant might also be liable for damages if it took the landlord some period of time, such as a month, to find a new tenant. In this case the first tenant would be liable for the month's rent if the landlord had made diligent efforts to find a new tenant.

If you are sued in Small Claims Court for an amount that seems excessive, simply go and tell the judge your side of the case and bring with you any witnesses and written documentation that help tell your story. If you are sued in Municipal Court, you may want to see a lawyer, especially if there is a lot of money involved (see Chapter 1, Part C).

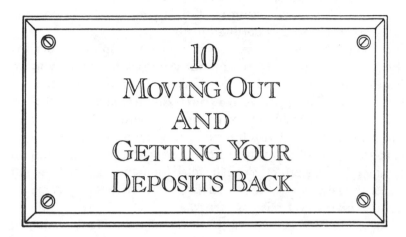

10
MOVING OUT
AND
GETTING YOUR
DEPOSITS BACK

Sooner or later the time comes to move on. Hopefully you are not leaving under fire, but on good terms. Maybe it's just time for some changes. The main concern at this point is with giving notice and getting back deposits which you put up at the outset.

A. GIVING NOTICE

Written notice of your intention to leave should be given in all situations. Oral notice is not legally adequate even if you have an oral rental agreement. Failure to give proper written notice can result in your being obligated to pay an extra month's rent. If you rent under **any** kind of document, read it carefully and see what it says about time and manner of giving notice. If it is silent on the subject, or if you have an oral agreement, then the time for notice is the same as the time between rent payments. If you pay rent once a month, you must give written notice of your moving date 30 days in advance. It is not necessary for your notice of departure to correspond to a due date for rent. That is, it would be proper to pay rent on March 1, give 30 days written notice of intention to move on March 10, and move out on April 9. (Of course, you would be obligated to pay the first 10 days of rent for April on April 1.) **Remember:** Keep a copy of all notices that you send for your file. If you have any reason to distrust your landlord, send the notice by registered or certified mail.

If you rent under a lease, you have made a contract to occupy the premises until the lease runs out. When the lease ends you are free to leave. California law does not require notice at the end of a lease, but **read the provision of your lease carefully:** you will likely find that it requires you to give a notice in writing 30 days before the lease runs out if you intend to leave, otherwise you will be regarded as automatically switching over to a month-to-month tenancy. This is perfectly legal if called for in the lease and will put you in the same position as if you had a "written rental agreement" as far as giving notice is concerned.

An example of a 30-day notice from the tenant to the landlord appears on the next page.

By the way, don't forget about your deposit of last month's rent. If you paid the last month's rent at the outset, apply it now, and refer to it in your letter.

B. GETTING YOUR DEPOSITS BACK

Be sure to read the discussion on deposits in Chapter 2, Part C.

One of the most common sources of dispute between landlords and tenants is over the return of deposits. Some landlords act as if deposits are part of the rent and try to return them as infrequently as possible. The legal rules are contained in Section 1950.5 of the California Civil Code and are very simple. Within two weeks after the tenant moves out, the landlord must return all cleaning and security deposits or "fees" that are not reasonably necessary to remedy tenant defaults, repair damages caused by the tenant (exclusive of normal wear and tear), or to clean the premises. If the landlord retains any of the tenant's deposits for these purposes, he or she must furnish (also within two weeks) the tenant with an

1500 Acorn Street #4
Cloverdale, California
April 10, 19_

Smith Realty Co.
10 Jones Street
Cloverdale, California

Dear Sirs:

As you know, I occupy Apartment #4 at 1500 Acorn Street.
This is a formal written notice of my intention to vacate
Apartment #4 at 1500 Acorn Street on May 12, 19__. I will, of
course, pay you the correct amount of rent on May 1, 19__ to
cover the period from May 1 to May 12, 19__.

I plan to leave the apartment clean and in good physical
condition and will appreciate the return of my security and
cleaning deposit promptly after I move out.

Yours truly,

Patricia Parker

itemized written statement of the basis for, and the amount of, any security received and the disposition of such security and shall return any remaining portion of such security to the tenant.

If a landlord acts in **bad faith** and does not return the money or properly account for any part that he keeps, he may be liable for up to $200 in punitive damages over and beyond the amount of the deposits unjustly retained. The burden of proof as to the reasonableness of the amounts claimed is on the landlord. However, many tenants who have been through Small Claims Court have told us that getting awarded all, or a part, of the punitive damage amount is extremely difficult. Some judges undoubtedly are biased in favor of landlords. How can you counter this bias where it exists? The best way to do it is to thoroughly prepare your case and document that the landlord's failure to return your deposits within fourteen days was not only a mistake, but was without any reasonable basis in fact. In addition, "bad faith" might also be shown by proof that the landlord has a practice of failing to return security deposits. This can often be done with the assistance of your local tenants' organization.

When you are about to move out, if you feel that your apartment has not been damaged beyond normal wear and tear, and if it is clean, you should take the following steps to protect yourself:

- If you filled out a landlord-tenant checklist when you moved in as discussed in Chapter 2G (or even if you didn't), it is also a good idea for you and your landlord to fill one out now;
- Just as you did when you moved in, you or a friend should take photographs of the apartment;
- Have some responsible people thoroughly check the dwelling so that they can, if necessary, testify on your behalf that it was clean and in good shape when you moved out;
- Keep as part of your permanent file all receipts for the purchase of cleaning materials that you use in your final clean-up.

If you are on good terms with your landlord, it makes good sense to invite him over when you get done cleaning to have him go over the place with you. This is the time to discuss particulars about the return of your deposits. If there is any damage, you can discuss a fair price for its repair. You might have already received estimates from repair people to show him.

RENT WITHHOLDING: If your premises are going to be left clean and undamaged, but you anticipate trouble recovering your deposit, there is one common technique available which tenants often employ. Though not technically legal, it can often work as a practical solution. Many people who are planning to move out of the area and will not have easy access to Small Claims Court adopt this technique because they have no other practical way to protect themselves. A month (or more if necessary) before the end of tenancy, add up all deposits, last month's rent, etc. and tell the landlord that you are applying it as rent. He won't be pleased with this approach, but by the time he can get into court you'll be packed up and gone and he will not be entitled to any damages as long as your place was left clean and in good repair. Legally, when you move out the landlord's duty to return the various deposits is set off against your duty to pay rent, so neither party is entitled to damages. It is unlikely that your landlord will take any action, but just in case make sure you have photographs and witnesses to attest to the condition of your place at the time you leave. If you decide to follow this procedure you should clearly explain to your landlord what you are doing in writing (see next page).

1500 Acorn Street #4
Cloverdale, California
March 28, 19___

Smith Realty Co.
10 Jones Street
Cloverdale, California

Dear Sirs:

   As you know, I occupy Apartment #4 at 1500 Acorn Street
and regularly pay rent to your office once a month.
   Please take note that this is a formal written notice of my
intention to vacate apartment #4 on May 1, 19___.
   In speaking to other tenants in this area I have learned that
from time to time the return of cleaning deposits has been
the subject of dispute between landlord and tenant. Accord-
ingly, I have decided on the following course of action:
Instead of sending you the normal $200 rent payment today, I
am sending you instead $50 and ask that you apply the $150
cleaning deposit to my last month's rent.
   I will leave the apartment spotless. If you should doubt this
or want to discuss the matter further please give me a call and
come over. I think that you will be satisfied that I am dealing
with you honestly and in good faith and that the apartment,
which is clean now, will be spotless when I leave.

                          Very truly yours,

                          Patricia Parker

   In most situations a letter such as this and perhaps a chat with the
landlord will clear the matter up. If the landlord gets hostile,
however, you may want to deposit the amount of the last month's
rent in a trust account at a local bank to be paid to the landlord
only after your deposits are returned. The chances of the landlord

taking you to court over this issue are very low. If he does, however, your letters and bank account, if you set one up, will be strong indications of your good faith and should be adequate to protect you.

MAKE A FORMAL DEMAND: If you do not use the rent withholding technique discussed above, and if after you vacate you can't get satisfaction from the landlord, you should make a written demand for the return of your money such as the one set out below.

1504 Oak Street #2
Cloverdale, California
October 15, 19___

Smith Realty Co.
10 Jones Street
Cloverdale, California

Dear Sirs:

As you know, until September 30, 19___, I resided in apartment #4 at 1500 Acorn Street and regularly paid my rent to your office. When I moved out I left the unit cleaner than it was when I moved in.

As of today I have received neither my $100 cleaning deposit not my $100 security deposit, nor have I received any accounting from you for that money. Please be aware that I know about my rights under California Civil Code Sec. 1951.5, and that if I do not receive my money within the next week, I will regard the retention of these deposits as showing bad faith on your part and shall sue you not only for the $200 in deposits, but for the $200 punitive damages allowed in Sec. 1951.5 of the California Civil Code.

May I hear from you soon.

Very truly yours,

Patricia Parker

If the letter doesn't produce results, you can consider seeing an attorney to have him contact the landlord for you. Sometimes his added authority is just right to scare the landlord into a response, and some lawyers are good negotiators. On the other hand, lawyers are expensive—make sure ahead of time exactly what the lawyer will do and how much it will cost.

SUE THE LANDLORD IN SMALL CLAIMS COURT: If the formal demand doesn't work, you should consider suing the landlord. If you rent under a lease or rental agreement which provides for the landlord's attorney's fees, then you, too, are entitled to attorney's fees if you win your law suit. In such situations you might ask an attorney to handle the matter for you. Be sure you thoroughly discuss his fee arrangements ahead of time.

In most cases, however, you should probably bring your own suit in Small Claims Court. The rules governing Small Claims proceedings are contained in the California Code of Civil Procedure, Section 116 et seq. The cost for filing papers and serving the landlord will not exceed $6.00. The best source of information on how to prepare and present a Small Claims Court case and collect your money if you win is **Everybody's Guide to Small Claims Court**, Warner, Nolo Press.

To sue your landlord in Small Claims Court, go to your local courthouse and find the Clerk of the Small Claims Court. Tell the Clerk you want to sue your landlord and she will give you a form "affidavit" to fill out. The Clerk is required by law to fill it out for you, if you so request. On the form, you must say how much you are claiming the landlord owes you. This amount cannot exceed $1500.* You figure the amount you want to claim by asking for the portion of the deposit the landlord owes you plus, if you have a chance of showing "bad faith," $200 in "punitive damages."** If this adds up to more than $1500, then you either have to waive the excess over $1500 or else not use the Small Claims Court. If you have to make this decision, you should consider that you may not easily win the full $200 in punitive damages.

---

*Small claims jurisdiction should be raised considerably. Also legislation should be enacted to set up a landlord-tenant court where disputes of all kinds could be settled cheaply and quickly without recourse to expensive lawyers.
**Small claims courts may award these punitive damages. Civil Code Section 1950.5(j).

After you file the form with the Clerk, she will send a copy of it to the landlord by registered or certified mail, with an order for him to appear in Court for a trial on the suit at a certain date and time. To find out that date and time, ask the Clerk. That date must be not less than 10 nor more than 40 days after the date of the order to appear, if the landlord lives within the county. If he doesn't live in the county, the date must be not less than 30 nor more than 70 days after the date of the order to appear (Code of Civil Procedure Section 116.4).

The trial is very informal. No lawyers are present and there are no formal rules of evidence. There is no jury. When you come to court for your hearing bring the file or envelope with your records. All papers or pictures that you believe help your case should be included. Also bring with you all witnesses who have first-hand information about the facts in dispute. If you do not have any experience with a court you can go down a day or two before and watch a few cases. You will see that it is a very simple procedure.

On the day your case is to be heard, get to the court a little early and check for your courtroom (referred to as a department). Sometimes this information is listed on sheets outside the department, tell the clerk or bailiff that you are present and sit down and wait until your case is called. When your turn comes, stand at the large table at the front of the room and tell the judge clearly what is in dispute.

Do not tell him a long story as he will get bored and possibly irritated. Remember, the judge hears many cases every day, and he will not be particularly excited about yours. If he gets bored he may stop listening and start thinking about what he is going to eat for lunch. Start your presentation with the problem and then give him **only** direct relevant facts. Be brief and to the point—don't ramble. You may show pictures and documents to the judge. When you are done with your oral presentation tell the judge you have witnesses and ask them to testify. The landlord will also have a chance to tell his side. You can expect it to be very different from yours, but stay cool! When he is done you may ask him questions if you feel that he has not told the truth or if he has left some things out. But often asking the landlord a lot of vague questions just gives him more opportunity to tell his side of the case. It is

especially important to **not** argue with the landlord or any of his witnesses—just get the facts out.

If you cannot speak English and cannot find a volunteer interpreter or afford to hire an interpreter, the court will probably be able to arrange for a volunteer for you.

EXAMPLE: In a case where a landlord has not returned your cleaning deposit after you have moved out and asked for it, you might present your case something like this: "Good morning Your Honor, my name is John Smith and I now live at 2330 Jones Street. From January 1, 19__ until January 1, 19__ I lived at 1500 Williams Street in a building owned by the Jefferson Realty Company. When I moved out the Realty Company refused to refund my $150 cleaning deposit even though I left the place spotless. I carefully cleaned the rugs, washed and waxed the kitchen and bathroom floors, washed, the inside of the cupboards and washed the windows. Your Honor, I want to show you some pictures that were taken of my apartment the day I moved out.* These were taken by Mrs. Edna Jackson who is here today and will testify. Your Honor, I don't have much else to say except that in addition to the amount of my deposit I am asking for $200 in punitive damages. I am entitled to these damages because I don't believe the landlord had any reason at all to withhold my deposits."** You would then ask your witness or witnesses to testify.

In most courts your witness will not take the witness stand but will remain at the table in front of the judge and will simply explain what he or she knows about the dispute. Typical testimony might go like this:

"Good morning, your honor. My name is Mrs. Edna Jackson and I live at 1498 Williams St. On January 1, 19__ when the plaintiff moved out I helped him move and clean up. The place was very clean when we finished. And just to show how clean it was, I took the picture that you were just shown. I'm sure those are the pictures I took because I signed and dated them on the back after they were developed."

---

*If you completed a checklist of the condition of the premises you will want to show it to the judge at this time.
**If you have any evidence that the landlord commonly withholds deposits with no good reason, be sure to introduce it.

NOTE: The above is meant only as a brief example to show you that being clear, concise and well-prepared is important. Often a judge will want to ask you questions. It is important not to be intimidated by the court process—usually the judge will be considerate and will help you if you get bogged down.

COMPLAIN TO LOCAL AUTHORITIES: If your landlord makes a habit of refusing to return security deposits to tenants, your local district attorney might sue him for fines and an injunction.* It never hurts to ask.

---

*See **People v. Sangiacomo** (1982) 129 Cal. App. 3d 364.

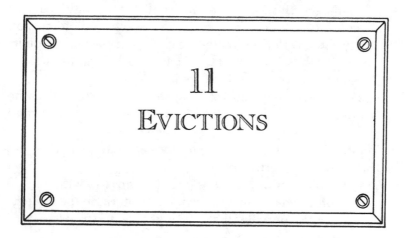

11
EVICTIONS

"Eviction" is the common term for the whole process that takes place when a landlord wants to force a tenant to get out. If the tenant fails to get out when he's told to, then the **only** thing the landlord can do, legally, is to go to court and bring an action called "unlawful detainer."

A. ILLEGAL LANDLORD CONDUCT

The law is clear in California that if a landlord wishes to evict his tenant, he must first go to court, giving the tenant prior notice of the court proceedings. He cannot take the law into his own hands by locking the tenant out, taking the tenant's belongings, taking off doors and windows, cutting off the utilities or any other kind of harrassment.

1. UTILITY CUT-OFF

California Civil Code Section 789.3 says that any landlord who causes any utility service (including water, heat, light, electricity, gas, telephone, elevator, or refrigeration) to be cut off with intent to terminate occupancy by a tenant is liable to the tenant for certain damages. This section applies whether the utility is paid for by the landlord or the tenant, and whether the landlord cuts off the utility directly "or indirectly" (e.g., by not paying the utility bill, presumably). This statute permits the tenant to sue the landlord and recover the following damages:

- Actual damages (e.g., meat spoiling in the refrigerator after the electricity was turned off, or, if the tenant has to leave because the utilities were turned off, motel bills);
- "Punitive" damages of up to $100 for each day or part thereof that a utility was turned off;
- A reasonable attorney fee (if the tenant wins the suit);
- A court order compelling the landlord to turn on the utilities;
- The statute also provides that the judge shall award at least $250 in damages.

2. LOCK-OUT

If the landlord locks you out, removes outside doors or window, or removes your personal property from your home with the intention of terminating your tenancy, he or she is in violation of Civil Code Section 789.3. The damages are the same as set out above for utility cut-offs. You can collect damages in Small Claims Court, but if you want quick action to get back into your home, see a lawyer, as the statute allows you to collect his or her fees. You might also call the police or district attorney, since these acts are crimes.* Even if the police won't cite the landlord, they may persuade him to let you in. Try very hard to get the police to at least write a report on the incident, as this may very well help in a later lawsuit against the landlord.

Tenants who live in "residential hotels" (apartment buildings which are called "hotels") are also protected against lock-outs.**

---

*Penal Code Sections 418 (Forcible Entry), 594 (Malicious Mischief) and 602.5 (Unauthorized Entry). Incidentally, it's illegal to evict a tenant in retaliation for making a criminal complaint. **Barela v. Superior Court**, 178 Cal.3d 618 (1981).
**Code of Civil Procedure Section 1159 and Civil Code Section 1940.

B. SUMMARY OF EVICTION PROCEDURE

If some unfortunate circumstances have brought you to the point where your landlord is ordering you to move, you need to stay calm and realize that nothing terrible is going to happen to you. While you are not in a desirable situation, it is not the end of the world. More than anything, you need to know your rights and how to exercise them.

When a landlord wants to force a tenant to leave he must follow a very strict legal procedure. The law **requires** him to proceed as follows:

1. He must have a legal reason for asking the tenant to leave. There are several circumstances that allow a landlord to bring an "unlawful detainer" action against a tenant. The most common are:

- Failure to pay rent when due;
- Failure to abide by some part of a lease or rental agreement such as keeping a pet when pets are specifically prohibited;
- Failure to leave a dwelling after the landlord has served a proper notice to vacate. Except in areas where tenants are protected by "for cause" eviction requirements, tenants without leases for a longer period may be given a 30-day notice to leave for any or no reason, so long as the reason or motive is not discriminatory under the Unruh Act or retaliatory because of the exercise of rights (see Chapter 7).

2. He must properly serve the tenant with a legally correct notice (more about this in part D);

3. He must start and win an unlawful detainer law suit (more about this in part D) in which the tenant:

- gets properly served with court papers,
- has a chance to file a legal response,
- is entitled to a court hearing.

4. After obtaining judgment he must secure an order from the court clerk authorizing the sheriff or marshal to actually evict the tenant (called a Writ of Restitution or Writ of Possession). This writ is then turned over to a peace officer. All of this can happen immediately in the case of municipal court judgments and after 20 days in the case of small claims judgments unless an appeal is filed. If a small claims appeal is filed, the tenant can't be evicted until the appeal is decided.

Five Day Final Warning: The Sheriff has no power to collect money from you, nor can he put you in jail for not paying rent. His job is to move you off the premises after he has been given a valid court order telling him to do so. Before he comes out to do this, he must deliver a final five day warning. He can give it to you personally, or tack it on the door and send another in the mail if no one is at home.

The Move: To say the very least, it would be foolish for you or your property to still be in the dwelling at the end of five days. At that time, anyone still there will be physically removed if they are named in the Writ of Possession and any of your (or their) possessions still on the property will be inventoried by the sheriff and turned over to the landlord. However, if a person is present when the peace officer comes to evict and the person **is not** named in the writ, but claims that they have resided there from before the time the landlord filed this action, the eviction may not proceed as to them. Instead, the landlord must go back to the court, obtain a special "show cause" order and give the person an opportunity to explain why he or she should not be evicted along with the persons named in the Writ of Possession (see Section D(2) of this chapter).

Of course, if after asserting your right to remain, the sheriff or constable insists on moving you out, do **not** resist or your next residence will be provided for free in the county jail. You are also subject to arrest if you return to the dwelling at any time after you are put out.

C. PLANNING WHAT TO DO

If you get a notice to vacate, you should sit down, relax, and think things over. Number one fact to importance is that you have plenty of time to to work it out—even if the landlord moves as fast as he can (and he probably won't), the very earliest that the Sheriff can show up is three weeks. Actually, it is very likely to take six weeks or longer. If you or your lawyer approach the case actively and negotiate or go into court, then the process can be slowed down a great deal.

One hard fact that you'll have to face is that unless you can get your landlord to change his mind about wanting you to leave, then eventually he can get you out. This means that no matter what else you do about the eviction, you ought to start looking for somewhere else to live.

When you are faced with an eviction, there are only a limited number of things you can do. You can:

- do nothing—just wait until you find another place, or the Sheriff comes, whichever happens first;
- negotiate with your landlord, either yourself or through your lawyer, to try to find a compromise solution to your problems and his;
- go into court (by yourself or with a lawyer) to make your case (and/or gain more time).

What you actually decide to do depends upon many considerations, including whether or not you have a good case, how easily you can get another place, how vulnerable you are to a money judgment, how much time and money you want to spend on your case and all the circumstances involved in your and your landlord's respective situations.

While you are making your plans, keep in mind that in addition to time it also costs a landlord a lot of money for his lawyer and for Sheriff's fees (the total cost to evict a tenant is often over $1000). If the landlord wins his unlawful detainer suit he will surely get a judgment against you for damages, but he then must go to the trouble of collecting the money. All of this normally makes a landlord reluctant to plunge into an unlawful detainer action if he can get you to move through persuasion. The high cost in time, trouble and money that the landlord faces gives you considerable leverage for negotiation.

If you don't pay your rent, then normally the landlord will do nothing for a few days except perhaps call you up to ask where the rent payment is. This is your chance to tell him what your situation is and try to work it out. Landlords vary enormously as to how long it takes them to start legal proceedings. This has nothing to do with the law, but a lot to do with psychology. Because it is expensive and time consuming to bring a legal action, most landlords hope that they will not have to do it. They hope that you will pay or leave voluntarily. It takes different landlords different lengths of time to come to the reluctant conclusion that the tenant is not going to pay the rent. Generally, the big landlord will move faster because he is used to evictions and knows just what to do, whereas the small landlord has to feel his way along.

If you are being evicted and don't want to leave you would be wise to get some help from a tenants' rights organization or perhaps an attorney. (See Chapter 1, Part C.) Consultation and advice from a lawyer need not be expensive and lawyers can often be helpful in negotiating with a landlord. For your information, and in case you cannot afford an attorney, the next section discusses some of the central technicalities of an eviction law suit and how to represent yourself.

D. REPRESENTING YOURSELF

Representing yourself is sometimes the only sensible alternative in landlord-tenant cases—lawyers cost too much. As we have said, lawyers can be helpful in many situations and often for a consul-tation. You will have to decide how much help you need and how much you can pay. But don't despair about representing yourself; thousands of people like you have managed it very well and often report that handling their own affiairs has given them a great deal of satisfaction.

1. NEGOTIATING A SETTLEMENT

Negotiating your own settlement is probably the thing that you are most competent to do, but **not** if you and your landlord can't speak to one another reasonably and logically. If he's mad at you, your job will be a hard one! Also, often times the landlord's attorney may think he can intimidate a layperson (you'll show him!) whereas he wouldn't be as likely to try this with another lawyer.

If you decide to do your own negotiating, start as soon as possible to communicate with your landlord. Get to know what his problems are and try to get him to understand yours. Then try to find a compromise solution that will solve both your problems.

The landlord's power lies in his threat to take you to court, get you thrown out and get a judgment against you for a lot of money. Your power lies in the fact that for him to do this costs him time and a lot of money. If the landlord understands your problems and thinks that you are sincerely trying to get out, or if you promise to get out by a certain date, then he would probably want to avoid the expense and hassle of a law suit by making a deal with you. If you have any claim at all to a good defense (see Part 3, below) you have a mighty weapon, for if you go to court with it, you can greatly increase the time of the eviction and expense to the landlord.

The range of possible deals is as wide as the numbers of cases—just try to do the best you can with your circumstances. Landlords have been known to go so far as to pay the tenant a little money to help him move, and forget the due bill, if the tenant will just get out quickly. In many cases such a solution can end up to be much cheaper for him in the long run. However, it would be more typical for the landlord to agree to drop the law suit in exchange for your agreement not to contest his eviction, to get out by a certain date and to pay a certain sum of money, presumably something less than he might otherwise win against you in court.

In some cases the landlord will not want to drop his law suit completely, but he may instead be willing to agree ahead of time to the kind of judgment he will seek.

If you can make a deal, it is absolutely essential that you have it in writing to protect yourself against mistakes and double-dealing. A letter from the landlord or his attorney clearly stating everything that was agreed to in detail is adequate. If you end up having to draw up the agreement yourself, you can use the example below as a guide. Use whichever parts apply to you or make up your own.

2. TECHNICAL INFORMATION

The material in this section is by no means complete. It is merely a summary of the more important technicalities involved in an eviction proceeding. Reading this section will help you understand eviction better, and give you basic information in the event that you decide to take your own case into court. If you really want to do a thorough job of researching eviction procedures, we strongly urge you to read **California Eviction Defense Manual** by Moskovitz, Honigsberg & Finkelstein. You should be able to find it in your County Law Library.

a. Notice Requirements

In order for a landlord to win an unlawful detainer action to evict a tenant he **must** start by serving the tenant with a written notice. Landlords usually know how to make and serve notices properly. If a landlord does it wrong, your remedy is to raise the defect as a technical basis. You then gain time, as the landlord will have to start all over again. This is a very strong point with which you or your lawyer can bargain for other concessions.*

Below is a brief summary of the technical rules regarding notice and service:

i. 3-day notices. If you are late with your rent in any amount, the landlord can serve you with a written notice to either pay up within three days **or** get out. The notice must describe the premises in question and state the amount of rent due. It must give

---

*At least one court in a confused decision has suggested that actual receipt of the notice by the tenant cancels out any technical mistake made in serving it. **Wilcox v. Anderson** (1978) 84 Cal.App.3d 593.

AGREEMENT

PATRICIA PARKER of 1500 Acorn Street, Apartment #4, Cloverdale, California, and SMITH REALTY CO., by their manager and authorized representative B. R. Smith, hereby agree as follows:

PATRICIA PARKER agrees:
(a) not to contest the unlawful detainer action brought against her by SMITH REALTY in Cloverdale Municipal Court;
(b) to leave the premises no later than _____;
(c) to pay to SMITH REALTY the sum of $_____, which sum when paid shall be full satisfaction for any and all obligations to SMITH REALTY, or agents, to date;
(d) *etc. . . .*

SMITH REALTY agrees:
(a) to drop the unlawful detainer action brought against PATRICIA PARKER in Cloverdale Municipal Court, Action #_____;
(b) to pay to PATRICIA PARKER the sum of $____ if she vacates the above premises no later than _____, 19 __;
(c) to seek judgment against PATRICIA PARKER for no more than $_____, said sum to be inclusive of all damages, attorneys fees and court costs;
(d) *etc. . . .*

_____   _____
Date   Smith Realty

_____   _____
Date   Patricia Parker

the tenant the choice of paying or leaving. This means that if the tenant pays the amount demanded within three days, then the notice is satisfied and is of no further meaning. Three day notices can also be given for other specific breaches of lease or rental agreements (i.e., loud parties or pets prohibited by the agreement). In each case the notice must specify the fault and demand its correction within three days as an alternative to moving out. Of course if no correction is made, you will only have to move if the court orders you to.

Counting the Three Days: To correctly count the three days, ignore the day on which the notice is served. Start counting with the next day and pay up by the end of the third day. If the third day falls on a Saturday, Sunday or court holiday, you have until the end of the next business day to pay up.

If the landlord accepts any amount of money at all from you after the notice is served he **may possibly** be required to start all over again with a new notice before going to court. The law is unclear on this point, but many municipal court judges have held that a landlord interrupts his own proceedings if he accepts part payments. See page 70 for additional information.

CAUTION: It sometimes happens that a three-day notice will be combined with a 30-day notice, all in the same document. In such cases, even if the tenant cures the fault such as paying the past due rent or getting rid of the dog within three days, he will still have to face the demand that he vacate in 30 days. If the combined notice is confusing, this may serve to invalidate either or both. Normally, 3 and 30 days are served to avoid the possibility of confusion. Read the notices carefully in any event.

ii. 30-day Notices. Except in rent control areas which offer "for cause" protection to tenants,* or when you have a lease for a longer period of time, a landlord may give you a 30-day notice to quit without any reason whatsoever. Remember, however, that an eviction may never be based on an improper motive such as discrimination or retaliation for exercise of a right. All 30-day notices must be in writing. They may be given anytime during a month. If the period between your rent payments is shorter

---

*In San Francisco, Los Angeles, Berkeley, Santa Monica, and several other areas, rent control ordinances have been enacted which allow the landlord to evict on a 30-day notice only for certain reasons specified in the ordinance. Among the reasons found in one or another ordinance are the landlord wanting to live in the place himself, failure to pay rent, violation of some provision of the lease or rental agreement, use of the apartment for an illegal purpose, maintaining a "nuisance," refusal to let the landlord in to make repairs or show the place to a prospective buyer, refusal to sign a new lease when the old one runs out, and subletting without the landlord's consent. For more details, turn to Chapter 15. Also, ask your city clerk for a copy of your area's rent control law so you can see the specific grounds on which the landlord may seek to evict you.

than a month, then the notice can give you that shorter period in which to leave.

iii. Proper Service of Notices. A three-day notice must be served on you in one of these ways: 1) handed to you personally; 2) handed to a fairly grown-up child on the premises **and** a copy sent to you by mail; or 3) the "nail and mail" method (i.e., posting it in a conspicuous place at your home **and** mailing a copy). However, "nail and mail" may not be valid for 3-day notices in Santa Clara County [Davidson v. Quinn 138 Cal.App.3d Supp. 9]. 30-day notices may be served by certified or registered mail as well as by any of the three methods described above. Regular first class mail **is not** considered valid legal service.

COMMENT: If you receive a three-day notice, you can comply with the demand to pay rent and that's the end of it. However, if you get a 30-day notice, there's no real choice—if you don't leave, you will have to face the landlord's next action, probably an eviction action. You can try to talk your way into staying, but if the landlord is set on getting you out, it is difficult to stay in peaceful possession of the premises, even in areas requiring cause for eviction under rent control ordinances. However, through negotiations and other strategies, much can still be accomplished. Offer some money. If a landlord accepts money as rent for a time period starting after the thirty day notice runs out, then the notice is nullified and he will have to start over again.

If you can't talk your way into staying, at least try to work out delays, returns of deposits and other concessions from the landlord. Some landlords have found it cheaper to pay tenants some money to move out rather than spend a large sum on legal action. This is especially true where you are being evicted because the building is being sold and must be delivered free of tenants. The enormous price which most rental properties command these days means that your landlord may be willing to pay handsomely if you move quickly and don't threaten his prospective deal.

If you get a notice, it is time to decide quickly what course of action to take. If you can, see a lawyer for advice.

b. The Law Suit

If, (1) you have been properly served with a three-day or 30-day notice, and (2) when the time is up you are still on the premises, then, and only then, the landlord is eligible to go to court.* Once the landlord goes to court, and if you lose, it will be **at least** several weeks and often much longer before the Sheriff actually comes to move you out.

The name of the law suit brought to evict a tenant is "unlawful detainer." Landlords will almost always bring this action in the local Municipal Court, but it is possible for it to be done in Small Claims Court **if** your tenancy is a month to month one and you are being evicted for failure to pay rent. Small Claims Court may be less expensive for the landlord, since at least initially no attorneys are involved. However, it may also take the landlord several months or more to actually get you out, since if you lose in the Small Claims Court, you have a right to a new trial in the Superior Court and the eviction is stayed until that trial is over. Also, you have a right to be represented by an attorney in the new trial as well as a right to a jury. For a good understanding of how the Small Claims process works, read **Everybody's Guide to Small Claims Court**, Warner, Nolo Press. In that book the author strongly recommends against the use of Small Claims Court by landlords desiring to evict a tenant because of the possibility of long delays.

i. The Landlord's Court Papers. The court action is started when the landlord (or his attorney) files an unlawful detainer "Complaint." The Complaint is a document which briefly states the case against you, asks the court to order you out, and for a judgment against you for a certain amount of money to cover past due rent, attorney's fees, court costs and other damages. It is proper for him to ask for attorney's fees **only** if you rented under a document which has a provision stating that attorney's fees are recoverable.** Landlords usually ask for treble damages (three times what you actually owe). They have a legal right to make this request if they claim that the tenant was guilty of malice or bad faith in not leaving sooner. In most cases the judge will use his discretion to limit damages to that amount actually incurred by the landlord unless he feels that the tenant is deliberately trying to use the legal process to harass or cheat the landlord.

When the unlawful detainer complaint is filed, the court automatically issues a "Summons." The Summons is a notice from the

---

*However, in **Wilcox v. Anderson** (1978) 84 Cal.3d 593, the Court of Appeals intimated that actual notice by a tenant would cure the defective service. It might be better not to rely on this point alone in defending against an eviction, unless it's the only one you have.

**If the lease or rental agreement provides for attorney's fees for the landlord, you are also entitled to attorney's fees if you win, under Civil Code 1717.

court telling you that the action has started and how much time you have to respond. In Municipal Court, the Summons will tell you that in order to contest the case you **must** file a written "Answer" within five days of the day you were served, unless you were served by "substituted service" in which case you have 15 days to file an answer.

ii. Serving the Court Papers. After filing his papers, the landlord **must** serve you with a copy of the Summons and Complaint. In Small Claims Court this can be done by handing them to you or by sending them to you via certified or registered mail. In Municipal Court the rules governing service are a little more strict. Here you must be handed the papers personally or a procedure known as "substituted service" must be followed. Under this method a tenant who can't be served personally after reasonably diligent effort can be served by leaving a copy of the complaint and summons in the hands of a person at least 18 years old at the tenant's home or business after telling that person what the papers concern. In addition, another copy of the complaint and summons must be mailed to the tenant.

iii. The Tenant's Answer. If the action is in Small Claims Court, you do not need to file a written answer in order to be heard—you need only show up at the time of the hearing. However, most unlawful detainer actions are in Municipal Court, and in such cases to get a chance to present your side you must file a formal written Answer within five days of receipt of the Summons and Complaint. (If the fifth day falls on a Saturday, Sunday or holiday, the answer is due on the next business day.) If "substituted service" was used, you are allowed 15 days in which to answer. In the answer you deny the errors in the landlord's Complaint, and raise your own defenses.

iv. The Court Hearing. If the case is uncontested, the landlord says his piece and wins. If there is a contest, the judge listens to both sides, then makes his judgment. If you don't show up and "default," the judge may not require a hearing and the landlord will automatically win. If you default but still want to be heard you must file papers immediately to have the default set aside. Necessary forms and instructions are contained in the California Eviction Defense Manual which is available at your local county law library. You will need to give a good reason to explain your default (e.g., you never were served with the landlord's papers) and will also have to claim that you have a good defense to the landlord's eviction action. Don't delay.

v. The Court Judgment. After the unlawful detainer complaint has been served on you, if you do not respond your landlord will get a default judgment against you. If you or your attorney respond and go to court you may still lose and get a judgment entered against you, but it will take at least several weeks longer. If you go to court and win, the judgment will be entered against your landlord.

c. Outline of an Eviction Law Suit

Here is a brief outline of the main possible procedural steps in an eviction law suit filed in a Municipal Court. Most, if not all, of the steps are too technical for you to handle yourself, but you should know all the possibilities.

The landlord (called the "plaintiff") files his complaint in court. He then has a process-server serve a copy of the complaint and summons on the tenant ("defendant"). Within five days after this, the tenant must file in court, (and serve a copy on the landlord's attorney by mail), one of the following documents: an "answer," which says that the allegations of fact in the complaint are not true; a "demurrer," which says that the complaint is not drawn up correctly in a legal, technical sense; a "motion to strike," which says that some of the allegations or demands for relief in the complaint are improper; or a "motion to quash" the service of summons, which says that the summons was not legally proper or was not served properly.

If a motion to quash is filed, the judge will hold a hearing on it and decide it in a week or two. If the judge grants this motion, the landlord must have the tenant served with process again, essentially starting all over again.

If the motion to quash is denied, the tenant's attorney may then file a demurrer or motion to strike, if there are grounds for one of these. It may take another week or two for the judge to hear and decide this. If a demurrer is sustained or a motion to strike is granted, the landlord's attorney will have to rewrite his complaint. If the demurrer is overruled or the motion to strike is denied, the tenant's attorney will be given a few days to file an answer to the complaint.

The answer may deny some of the allegations of fact in the

complaint. It may also raise certain "affirmative defenses," which say that even if the allegations in the complaint are true, there are additional facts which require the court not to evict the tenant. These may involve such things as fraud in making the lease, racial discrimination, retaliatory eviction and breach of the "implied warranty of habitability."

Either side may request a jury trial if he puts up a deposit for jury fees (about $60, recoverable from the losing party) or gets the judge to allow him to proceed "in forma pauperis." Otherwise, the judge will hear and decide the facts. Eviction cases have "precedence" over other civil cases, and usually the trial will take place about 20 days after the answer is filed.

Before the trial, either attorney may engage in "discovery" — that is, trying to find out what evidence the other side has to prove their case and what he can get him to admit. This may be done by "written interrogatories"* or by a "deposition" at which the other party must come and answer questions under oath. A "motion to produce" may also be used, if you want to look at documents in the other party's possession.

After the answer has been filed and—in some courts—after all discovery has been completed, the landlord may file a memorandum that the case is "at issue," i.e., ready for trial. The clerk must then assign a trial date for within the 20 days after the "at issue" memorandum is filed.**

At the trial, the landlord's attorney puts on his case, having witnesses testify as to the facts. The tenant's attorney may cross-examine them. Then the tenant's attorney puts on his witnesses and the landlord's attorney then cross-examines them. Then each attorney makes an argument, and the jury or judge decides the case.

If the landlord wins, the tenant can appeal, but whether he can stay in possession during the appeal is up to the trial court judge, who might well condition such a "stay" on the tenant's paying the rent.

If the tenant wins, he obtains a judgment requiring the landlord

---

*You may obtain *form* interrogatories for unlawful detainer cases from the court clerk. Their use by either side is optional. See Appendix 3, page 219.

** If the tenant needs an extension of the trial beyond the date set by the clerk, two steps are required. First you must convince the court an extension is needed. This is done by filing a written application for extension complete with a declaration setting forth good reasons. If you vacate before the trial date, you are entitled to an automatic extension as to all remaining issues [Fish Construction Co. v. Moselle Coach Works (1983) 148 Cal.App.3d 654]. If the judge finds at a hearing that there is a reasonable probability the landlord will prevail at trial you will also be required to deposit future rent payments with the court as a condition of getting the extension. See Code of Civil Procedure 1170.5.

to pay his court costs and, if the lease or rental agreement provided for attorney's fees for either side, attorney's fees.

If the landlord wins, he will receive a "judgment" for (1) unpaid rent or, if the tenant refused in "bad faith" to pay rent or get out, up to three times the unpaid rent, (2) his court costs, (3) his attorney's fees, if the lease or rental agreement so provided, and (4) a "writ of restitution" for the premises.

If the tenant failed to file an answer on time, the landlord would obtain a "default judgment" containing all of these things without the tenant having a chance for a trial (unless the tenant quickly filed and was granted a "motion to set aside" the default and default judgment).

The landlord takes his judgment to the civil division of the county sheriff's office. If he deposits certain sheriff's fees (which are added to the judgment), the sheriff will "execute" the money part of the judgment by attaching the tenant's wages or bank account. He will execute the writ of restitution by serving a "notice to vacate" on the tenant. This requires the tenant to move out in five days. If he does not, the sheriff will come out and physically evict him.*

All of these procedural devices are more fully explained in the **California Eviction Defense Manual** (available in your County Law Library), which also contains forms for using them.

3. DEFENDING YOURSELF

In the second part of this section we discuss how to defend yourself in Small Claims Court. However, as we've already said,

---

*In the case of **Arietta v. Mahon** (1982) 31 Cal.3d 381, the California Supreme Court has prohibited sheriffs or marshals from evicting any adult 1) who is physically present when the eviction is being carried out, 2) who claims residency from before the date the unlawful detainer action was filed, and 3) who is not actually named in the document which instructs the sheriff or marshal to evict (called a Writ of Possession or Writ of Execution). This often happens when the landlord is unaware of roommates or sublessees who may not be tenants as such but who live there nonetheless. If you are such a person and advise the sheriff or marshal of your claims, they in turn must inform the landlord of your presence and the landlord must serve you with a notice of another court hearing (called an order to show cause) wherein you will have a chance to tell the judge why you shouldn't be evicted. Of course, you will be evicted unless you can claim some legitimate status as a tenant (see Chapter 3).

most unlawful detainer suits are filed in Municipal Courts, so the major part of our attention is there.

a. In Municipal Court

Defending yourself in a municipal court can be complicated. Unfortunately, some judges simply do not give laypeople (especially low-income people) the respect that they give lawyers. It is a sad commentary on our laws that it is so hard for ordinary folks to speak for themselves, especially if you consider that this condition is not really necessary.*

If you still want to go ahead and represent yourself, it is your right to do so. Many others have managed it very successfully. We are only going to show you how to file a simple answer which will get you into court. You may have other remedies, but they are beyond the scope of this book. If you desire to defend your case in a more sophisticated manner, making legal motions and raising affirmative defenses, go to a law library and ask to see the **California Eviction Defense Manual** by Moskovitz, et al. This book contains information and authorities on the various procedures and defenses, with copies of the relevant statutes and useful forms.

Your answer must be filed within five days after you are served with court papers (if the fifth day falls on a weekend or holiday, file it on the next business day.)

There are two methods to use to file your answer in Municipal Court:

Method 1: Prepare a traditional typed pleading (original and three copies) on numbered legal type paper (available at any stationery store) by following the instructions on the proceeding pages.

Method 2: Use the preprinted form entitled Answer—Unlawful Detainer available free from the Municipal Court Clerk. See Appendix 2 for instructions.

---

*Most, if not all eviction actions could and should be taken out of Municipal Court and assigned to a "landlord-tenant" court. This would involve simplifying many archaic procedural rules and reducing the need for lawyers.

```
 1   Your name _____
 2      Address _____
 3              _____
 4      Phone _____
 5   Defendant, in pro per
 6
 7
 8
 9            MUNICIPAL COURT OF THE STATE OF CALIFORNIA
10    ▭ ➝ _____
11
12   _____ ,
13             Plaintiff(s)          No. ___ ← ③
14        vs.
15   _____ ,            ANSWER
16            Defendant(s)
17
18            Defendant(s) answer the complaint as follows:
19
20                          I              ④↓
21        Admit the allegations contained in paragraph(s)_____ , _____ ,
22   and _____ [of the 1st Cause of Action, and paragraph(s)_____ ,
23   _____ and _____ of the 2d Cause of Action].
24
25                          II
26        With the exception of the admisisons set forth above, defendant(s) deny
27   each and every, all and singular, generally and specifically the allegations
28   contained in paragraph(s) _____ , _____ and _____ [of the 1st Cause
29   of Action, and paragraphs _____ , _____ and _____ of the 2d Cause
30   of Action].
31
32        WHEREFORE Defendant(s) pray that Plaintiff(s) take nothing by this
```

action; that defendant(s) recover costs of suit including reasonable attorneys fees; and for such other relief as may be deemed just.

⑥ ⟶ _____
                                    Defendant

_____
                                    Defendant

VERIFICATION

I am (a) defendant in the above action; I have read the foregoing Answer, and know the contents thereof; and I certify that the same is true of my own knowledge.

I certify, under penalty of perjury, that the foregoing is true and correct.

Executed on _____ _[date]_ _____, 19 __, at _____ _[place]_ _____, California.

⑦ ⟶ _____
                                    Defendant

PROOF OF SERVICE BY MAIL

I am a citizen of the United States and a resident of the county of _____, I am over the age of 18 years and not a party to the above action; my residence address is: _____ , California. On_____ , 19 __, I served the within Answer on the Plaintiffs in said action by placing a true copy thereof enclosed in a sealed envelope with postage thereon fully prepaid, in the United States post office mail box at_____ _[city]_ _____, California, addressed as follows: ⟵ **⑧**

_____

I, _____ _[name of sender]_ _____ , certify under penalty of perjury that the foregoing is true and correct. Executed on _____ _[date]_ ____, 19 __, at__ _[city]_ , California.

⑨ ⟶ _____
                                    [signature]

1. Type in the title of the court, exactly as it appears on the Complaint.

2. Type in the names of the parties, exactly as it appears on the Complaint.

3. Don't forget to type in the number of the case. Get it from the Complaint.

4. Read the Complaint very carefully and type in here the number of each paragraph which you can agree with completely. Do not list here any paragraph which has anything in it with which you do not agree. If there is more than one Cause of Action in the Complaint, continue as shown by the words within the parentheses.

5. Type in the number of each paragraph of the Complaint which has anything in it with which you do not agree. Use the words in the parentheses if there is more than one cause of action.

6. The Answer must be signed by each person who has been named by the Complaint, because any person not signing has not answered and may lose by default.

7. Any one of the defendants can sign the Verification. Type in the date and place where signed.

8. Enter here the name of the landlord or his attorney, as it appears in the upper left of the first page of the Complaint.

9. Signature of person mailing Answer to plaintiffs.

It is important that the Answer be signed by **all** of the named defendants. The Verification need only be signed by any one defendant. The "Declaration of Service by Mail" must be signed by someone who is **not** a defendant and who is a citizen over the age of 18.

After you prepare your Answer and Declaration, have one copy mailed to the landlord's lawyer (or, if he has none, to the landlord) and keep the other copies. Take the original to the office of the Clerk of the court in which the complaint was filed. To file it, you will have to pay a filing fee. How much this is depends on how many defendants there are. It will probably be between $10 and $25, payable by cash or money order only.

A few days after you file your answer, you will probably receive a notice from the Clerk of the court telling you when the trial will be. On the day of the trial, make sure you show up on time, ready to prove your case, **with any witnesses you have**. (Letters or other documents will probably not be accepted unless they are from the landlord or his agent. You must have "live testimony.")

When you get to the trial, here are some of the possible defenses you might raise, if they fit your case and if you can prove them:

1. In cases where the Complaint is based on a three-day notice:
- you did not get a three-day notice;
- notice failed to specify the correct amount of rent overdue;
- notice failed to give you the alternative of paying up (or stop violating lease) **or** getting out;
- notice did not state "clearly and unequivocally" that you are to get out if you don't pay up or quit violating lease;
- notice served on you before rent actually due;
- the amount of rent demanded was incorrect because you agreed on a different rent with the landlord;
- the complaint was served on you before the three days (from the date of service of the three-day notice) ran out;
- although the complaint says you violated the lease or rental agreement, it did not tell you which provision;
- the landlord accepted rent after giving you the three-day notice;
- the landlord materially breached his "implied warranty of habitability" (see section on rent withholding in Chapter 6); or, if you live in a city with a rent control ordinance and the landlord is trying to evict you without one of the "good cause" reasons allowed in your city's rent regulation ordinance.

Here is a way your answer might raise this issue: After you deny the landlord's statements as discussed on previous pages and before the paragraph entitled WHEREFORE, type:

Affirmative Defense—Breach of
Implied Warranty of Habitability

I

Defendant admits that he failed to pay the amounts of rent

alleged in the complaint to have been due. Defendant alleges, however, that said rent was not due and owing, because during the period for which rent was allegedly due, plaintiff was in violation of the implied warranty of habitability.

II

During such period, plaintiff was required by law to substantially comply with certain housing code provisions, but failed to do so, in the following respects. (Now specify each defect. For example:) The toilet constantly leaked water onto the bathroom floor, and the premises have been infested with cockroaches.

III

Plaintiff had knowledge of said conditions and a reasonable time to correct them, but he failed to do so.

IV

Said defective conditions were not caused by the wrongful conduct or abnormal use of the premises by defendant or any person under his authority.

V

Because of said defective conditions, the reasonable rent for the period for which plaintiff is claiming rent due is zero. Therefore, plaintiff is entitled to no rent whatsoever and is not entitled to evict for nonpayment of said rent.

---

2. In cases where the complaint is based on a 30-day notice:
- you did not get one;
- the 30-day notice did not "clearly and unequivocally" tell you to get out at the end of 30 days;

- the complaint was filed before the 30 days ran out;
- the landlord accepted rent for a period of time beyond the 30-day notice.

3. Other defenses:

- although the complaint asks for "treble damages" because you allegedly refused to move "in bad faith" or "willfully held over," you had good reasons for being unable or unwilling to move;

    NOTE: Since most complaints ask for treble damages, this defense is your most certain justification for filing an Answer and going to court. Even if you have no other valid defense, it is reasonable to go to court to try to avoid treble damages (and, in the process, you get more time before the Sheriff comes).

- the landlord is trying to evict you because of your race; reason prohibited under the Unruh Act (see Chapter 5).

- the landlord is trying to evict you in retaliation for your reporting code violations to a city agency, for organizing other tenants, for legally withholding rent, or for using your "repair-and-deduct" remedy or for any other exercise of your lawful rights. Civil Code Section 1942.5.

If the judge or landlord's lawyer says that you are being too "technical" by raising these defenses, point out that because the landlord is trying to take your home, the law requires him to **strictly comply** with the rules before he can evict you.*

If you have any questions or problems with preparing your answer or with other court procedures, go see the Clerk of the court. Clerks are sometimes quite helpful (and sometimes they're not!).

NOTE: If you wish to make affirmative defenses you may find it easier to use the pre-printed Answer form in Appendix 2.

b. Small Claims Court

Many landlords prefer to bring their eviction law suits in Small Claims Court, rather than regular Municipal Court. Since the procedures are easier, the landlord can handle the case himself and save the expense of hiring a lawyer. Since lawyers are not allowed in Small Claims Court, the landlord doesn't have to worry about the tenant having a lawyer to fight for him.** However,

---

*__Horton-Howard v. Payton__, 44 Cal. App. 108, 112; 186 Pac. 167 (1919).
**However, the tenant can obtain a new trial if the landlord wins in Small Claims court and is entitled to a lawyer as well as a stay of the eviction pending the outcome. Read on!

while an attorney cannot represent you in Small Claims Court, he can advise you on how to represent yourself.

If you want to look them up, the rules regarding Small Claims Court are mostly contained in the California Code of Civil Procedure, Sections 116 et seq. and are summarized in **Everybody's Guide to Small Claims Court**, Warner, Nolo Press.

The landlord can use Small Claims Court to evict you only if (1) the term of your tenancy is no longer than month-to-month and (2) the amount of rent or damages he claims does not exceed $1500, and (3) you are being evicted for failure to pay rent.

The landlord begins his law suit in Small Claims Court by filing an "affidavit" which sets out what he is alleging and demanding. The Clerk of the court then mails a copy of this to the tenant, with an order setting the date and time for trial, which will usually be 10 to 30 days later.

At the trial, the landlord presents his case and then you present your case. You and your witnesses testify under oath. Formal rules of evidence do not apply. Nevertheless, you should be prepared to present your case persuasively, smoothly and quickly. Small Claims Court judges are usually able to allow only a few minutes for each case. Do **NOT** try to argue with the landlord or his witnesses. Be cool and just present your own side as clearly as you can.

For possible defenses to raise, look at the list in the above section.

After the trial, the judge will usually take the case "under submission," and will notify the parties of his decision in a few days by postcard.

If the landlord loses, he cannot appeal. He is all through. If he still wishes to evict you, he will have to find new grounds for doing so.

If the landlord wins, he will receive a judgment like the one he would get in regular Municipal Court, except that the money part cannot exceed $1500. The judgment **cannot** be turned over to the Sheriff during the 20 days after judgment is entered. During this time, you may file a **notice of appeal** to the Superior Court. If you file a notice of appeal during this period, the case is transferred to the Superior Court, where you will receive a brand new trial (a "trial de novo") and may have an attorney. Until that trial, execution of the judgment against you is automatically stayed (C.C.P. Section 117j).

Note that, unlike the appeal from a regular Municipal Court judgment, where a stay of execution is in the "discretion" of the trial court judge, this stay is automatic, and no bond or other conditions can be placed on the stay. For this reason, the fact that the landlord uses the Small Claims Court **can** be more useful to **you** than to him. If you win there, you win, and if you lose there, you get a new chance in Superior Court, and the landlord loses a lot of time. You get this, however, only if you file your notice of appeal on time. Therefore, **if you lose a Small Claims Court case, see an attorney right away**, so he can file the notice of appeal and represent you in the new trial in Superior Court.

If the tenant loses in Superior Court, an attorney's fee of $15 will be added to the judgment against him, and the judgment may then be executed.

E. AFTER THE EVICTION

1. THE LANDLORD CAN TRY TO COLLECT MONEY DAMAGES
The landlord's judgment will almost certainly include an award for a sum of money. Once he gets you out, he can try to collect this money. He can garnish your wages if you work, or he can go after your bank account or any valuable property you have which is not covered by California exemption laws.* If the Sheriff or Marshall locked up any of your property when he moved you out, the landlord can definitely **not** satisfy his judgment out of this property.

2. YOU CAN TRY TO GET YOUR PROPERTY BACK

When the Sheriff or Marshall inventories your property, it is then turned over to the landlord. Usually, he will put it into storage. The landlord must hold the property for at least 15 days

---

*If you are having debt problems we recommend **California Debtors' Handbook– Billpayer's Rights**, Warner and Honigsberg, Nolo Press. See advertisement at back of this book.

before putting it up for sale. During this time, you can redeem your property simply by paying storage costs. Even if the property is lawfully sold, the landlord still may not keep any amount above the storage costs. You are entitled to the rest. If the landlord violates the rules, you should see a lawyer, or consider suing him in Small Claims Court. The Small Claims Court has the power to order your property returned, or you can sue for its monetary value up to $1,500. If you are in this situation, see Section 1174 of the Code of Civil Procedure.

3. A SECOND CHANCE

After a tenant is ordered evicted by a court, he or she may apply to the same court under Code of Civil Procedure Sec. 1179 to have the eviction order set aside on grounds of hardship. If the application is granted, the tenant must then pay all rent due, or comply with whatever provision of the lease or rental agreement was involved in the eviction in the first place.

12
TENANTS
ACTING TOGETHER

So far in this book all of the solutions to tenants' problems have been discussed for the tenant acting alone. Acting alone is not nearly as likely to produce results as is acting together with other people, but people on their own resources is the rule these days rather than the exception. This chapter is about methods and techniques by which tenants can gather themselves together and organize to deal with the landlord and law makers, but all the organization in the world is not worth one bit of neighborliness— and the organization is not nearly as likely to succeed without it.

In many places in California it feels like people have forgotten what "neighbor" means, and how to be good neighbors to one another. Neighborliness is based upon caring, understanding and need. if you have caring and understanding in your heart, you don't need any of this mundane advice anyway. What about needs? If an intruder is sneaking into your place and you yell for help, it would be good if someone came running. If Mrs. Jones next door is sick, maybe you could take her some soup or help with the kids—who knows when you will need the favor returned? And favors are not always returned by the same people who owe you, but what matter, so long as the accounts roughly balance?

Help her. If your washer breaks, maybe someone in the block knows how to fix it, and maybe they'd like some of your famous pie! If all you local folks get together you can have fun. You can take turns taking all the kids to a ball game or have a picnic. You can buy food at wholesale every other week and distribute it. And woe to the landlord who tries to mess with anyone in a unit full of people that get along together and who have read this book!

A. TENANT ORGANIZING

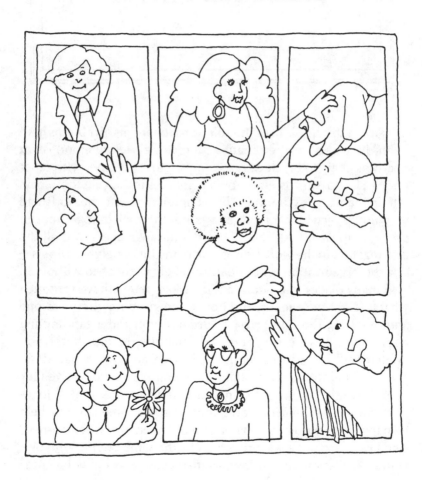

As we have seen, the odds in favor of an individual tenant getting an unreasonable landlord to be more reasonable are low. The landlord has most of the power. Not only is state law heavily weighted in his favor, but he normally has far more in the way of financial resources than does the tenant. Most landlords can afford attorneys—most tenants cannot. As long as tenants are divided he can deal with each one separately and will almost always come out on top.

In many ways the landlord/tenant situation in the 1980's is similar to the labor/management situation of 1900. At the turn of the century one worker without a union had little chance of getting better working conditions or wages from a giant corporation. Indeed, a worker who showed the bad sense to make such a request would probably be walking the bricks in a big hurry. While one tenant dealing with a small landlord **may** be able to work out a sensible relationship as neither party has a great deal more power than the other, the individual tenant dealing with the large landlord has little real chance of influencing his situation very much. In fact, he is in much the same situation as was the worker before unions came on the scene. The bigger the business, the more it is run like a machine, the more humanity is forced out. The tenant either conforms to the hundreds of rules in the lease and lets his rent be raised whenever it suits the landlord, or he is out on the street trying to find another place that will probably be just as bad. This is supposed to be a "free country." Pity the poor tenant who is given life by God and freedom by the United States Constitution, only to have most of it impaired by the standard form lease. Of what value is all your freedom if the only place you can find to live will not let you have a pet, a baby, a party or hang a picture on the wall. As one tenant remarked recently, "The only thing I can do in my apartment is sleep—and if I snore, I'm in trouble."

There is a way to restore the balance of power in landlord/tenant relationships, at least to some degree. It involves getting tenants together and bargaining with the landlord as a group.

A tenant organization begins as a group of tenants who want to change their relationship with their landlord. This can involve forcing him to make repairs, stopping a rent increase, or stopping arbitrary treatment of tenants. The tenant organization may fight the landlord and force him to sign an agreement—called a collective bargaining agreement—giving the tenants all or some of what they demand. If the tenant organization is together enough, it will also force the landlord to deal with it on a continuing basis.

To understand why a tenants' organization can work, consider the material in Chapter 1, Part B. As we discussed there, the landlord business normally operates so that the landlord has very little of his own cash tied up in the building or buildings that he claims to own. Most of the time he is simply taking money from tenants in the form of rent, giving it to the bank in the form of mortgage payments and the City in the form of taxes, and pocketing the difference. To pay his bills the landlord is dependent upon the majority of his tenants paying the rent. While he can easily deal with a few tenants who hassle him, he is not equipped to handle any sort of concerted tenant action. If all of a sudden no one pays the rent he is in real trouble. He can, of course, bring an "unlawful detainer" against every tenant, but this is extremeley expensive. In the meantime, he is getting no rent for a considerable period of time and his bills are piling up.

Just as to a labor union the ultimate weapon is the ability to strike, so, too, the strike is the ultimate sanction possessed by a tenants organization. This does **not** mean, however, that the strike should be used often. Many labor unions rarely strike. They don't need to. They are well organized and able to negotiate from strength. Sensible management will normally accept the fact that people have gotten together and be willing to negotiate a liveable contract. Tenants, like union members, should work to create a sound, well supported organization that can negotiate from strength and which seeks to arrive at understanding rather than conflict.

Tenant organizations are usually set up in a crisis situation, when some dispute arises. This is not always the case, however. Even when no dispute is going on, a tenant organization can be a good way for neighbors to get together to organize social activities, baby-sitting cooperatives, wholesale food purchases, and the like, as well as to establish a group to deal with the landlord when problems arise.

This chapter will give you some ideas on how to set up a tenant organization, tactics to use in pressuring the landlord, and how to negotiate a good agreement with him. Keep in mind, however, that a **tenant organization is only as effective as the will of its members and leaders to make it effective**. This takes time, energy, patience, and the willingness to take risks. Most of all, it takes a sense of community, understanding and identity between the tenants. Knowing techniques may be helpful, but it cannot replace these essential qualities. If you feel that these qualities are not there and cannot be inspired, you probably should give up the idea of forming a tenant organization. Read the opening paragraphs of this chapter one more time, then find some way of dealing with the landlord by yourself.

There are a number of local organizations in California actively organizing and giving advice to tenants. Unfortunately, because of lack of funding, tenants' rights groups have a hard time sustaining themselves. In the past we have tried to print a list of local organizations here, but because groups come and go so fast, it is no longer practical to try to print an exhaustive list. You should be able to get accurate, up-to-date information as to whether a tenants' organization exists in your area from one of the offices listed below, many of which belong to the California Housing Action and Information Network (CHAIN):

CHAIN
(Statewide Central Office)
P.O. Box 20226
Oakland, CA 94620
(415) 653-6315

SANTA BARBARA TENANTS' UNION
331 N. Milpas, #C
Santa Barbara, CA 93103
(805) 965-0822 or
(805) 962-3660

OAKLAND EVICTION DEFENSE CTR
1440 Broadway
Oakland, CA 94612
(415) 763-5320

WESTSIDE FAIR HOUSING
COUNCIL
10835 Santa Monica Blvd., #203
Los Angeles, CA 90025
(213) 475-9671

BERKELEY TENANTS' ACTION PROJECT
2022 Blake Street
Berkeley, CA 94704
(415) 843-6601

SAN FRANCISCO
TENANTS' UNION
558 Capp Street
San Francisco, CA 94110
(415) 282-6622

COMMUNITY HOUSING SERVICE
Warren House, #53
Humboldt State University
Arcata, CA 95521
(707) 826-3824

B. SETTING UP A TENANTS' ORGANIZATION

1. GET THE TENANTS TOGETHER AT A MEETING

Two or three concerned tenants can start a tenants' organization, if they are willing to do the work.

First, set a meeting time and place. Both should be convenient for most of the tenants.

Next, contact the tenants and ask them to come to the meeting. If you can possibly afford the time, do this in person, door-to-door. Recruit other tenants to help you. Use posting or distribution of notices only as a last resort or as a supplement to personal contact. If there are different races or ethnic groups in the building, try to get someone from each group to do the initial contacting of his or her own people.

2. THE FIRST MEETING

The first meeting should be conducted informally. People should get to know each other. They should be encouraged to speak about problems they have had with the building or the landlord. This way they will see what problems they have in common.

After this, explain to people the possibilities of collective action. Through reading this Handbook, you have seen how the law and the "market-place" are stacked against the tenant if he tries to deal with the landlord **individually**, but effective use of tactics described in this chapter can get greater gains **if the tenants act as a group**. Explain some of these tactics to them and use the labor union analogy. Explain that the tenants can also work out child care, wholesale food purchases, parties and the like, if they can learn to act together.

Next, try to deal with tenants' **fears**. People will be afraid of being evicted if they fight the landlord. Even if not expressed, these fears are there, so you had better try to bring them out and deal with them, or else you will find the tenants promising now but dropping out later when the action starts.

Explain to the tenants that while some tactics (such as the rent strike) involve a high risk of eviction, others (such as picketing) do not, if the group has a competent lawyer to protect it from retaliatory evictions (which are prohibited by law). It will be up to the group to decide which tactics to use, after a lawyer comes to talk to them. Explain that no action will be taken until the group is ready, having first figured out a strategy, elected leaders, made work assignments, and lined up legal representation and community support. Tell them, however, that there is always some risk of eviction or rent raise, and if anyone is not willing to take it, he had better drop out now so the others don't depend on him.

From the very beginning, try to deal with the problem of internal dissension. Among the group, there are very likely to be feuds, jealousies, and even racial and ethnic prejudices. Try to bring these out in the open and resolve them as soon as possible, or else they will keep the group from working together when the going gets tough.

3. SETTING UP THE ORGANIZATION

At the first meeting, if you feel that the tenants have the qualities needed to take on the landlord, set up the organization of the tenant union. You might elect officers, including a president, vice president, secretary and treasurer. Or, you might elect a "steering committee" of four or five members (with a chairperson) to be responsible for running things.

In setting up an organization, the most important thing is to see that there is a definite person responsible for each job which is important to the group. Here are some of the jobs that will need to be done: (1) line up a lawyer, (2) coordinate publicity, (3) get support from other groups, (4) handled the finances, (5) coordinate communication among the tenants (set up further meetings, contact people, etc.), (6) draw up demands and run negotiations, (7) gather information on the landlord. Each of these jobs can be assigned to a committee chairperson, or they can be handled by certain officers. The actual work on these jobs should be done by as many people as possible, so everyone feels involved and no one feels overburdened. But make sure that there is one person responsible for seeing that each job gets done, and that the chairperson or president is responsible for seeing that they get the job done.

Before adjourning the first meeting, the group should (1) select a name (for example, "540 Alcatraz Ave. Tenants' Union"), (2) decide the time and place of the second meeting, and (3) assign to specific people the jobs needed to be done before the second meeting, such as lining up a lawyer and contacting other tenants.

4. THE SECOND MEETING

The second meeting of the tenant union should be devoted to planning a strategy. Get some agreement on what are the most serious problems the tenants want resolved. Then have your "information" chairperson report on what he found out about the landlord and to which tactics the landlord might be most vulnerable. Then the lawyer should explain the possible consequences of using certain tactics and what he can do to protect the tenants.

Make sure that both the lawyer and the tenants understand that the lawyer is there only to give advice and to help protect the tenants. He is not there to make decisions for the group—only to supply necessary information to allow the group to choose a sensible course of action. If you get a lawyer who wants to run everything, get another. Also, see that tenants do not ask the lawyer to help solve their individual problems. He is there for the group, not for individuals, and if people fall back into an "individual" rather than "group" way of trying to solve problems, the tenant organization will fail.

Then the group should formulate a strategy. Make sure that there is general agreement with whatever strategy you decide on. A simple majority vote will not do if there is strong minority feeling opposed to it.

After the strategy is formulated, make specific work assignments to specific people, with deadlines for reporting to the chairperson or the group that the job is done.

5. CONTACT OTHER GROUPS

Whatever strategy you decide on, you should try as soon as possible to get support from other groups in the community. Churches, labor unions, political clubs and social clubs can furnish money, publicity, political influence and moral support. Ask each tenant what groups he has contacts with which might help.

Be sure to contact groups which are concerned with tenants' rights. Some cities now have city-wide tenant associations. They can furnish technical advice as well as publicity and moral support.

You should also contact California Housing Action and Information Network (address in *Introduction*). It is made up of tenants and tenant organizations from all over the state. CHAIN holds regional conferences, where tenants and specialists in tenant organization and tactics come together to gain political reform of landlord-tenant laws to deal with specific problems. It also sends out a newsletter, called "CHAIN Letter," which tells what tenant groups around the state are doing. The newsletter may give your organization some good ideas.

6. HOW MANY TENANTS DO YOU NEED BEFORE ACTING?

There is no set number. Sometimes only a few tenants will join initially, but many others may come in when the word spreads that the group is doing something and not just talking. If you cannot get a lot of people at first, try to get some "key" people who will influence others and bring them in later.

Obviously, the more tenants you have with you the more pressure the landlord will feel, so try to get as many tenants as you can in your tenant union.

C. GETTING INFORMATION ON THE LANDLORD

In order to find out how to deal with the landlord, you will need information on him. Sometimes you need to find out who the owner is. You should try to find out what his financial situation is like to see where he is most vulnerable. You need to know something about his personality before you negotiate with him.

Here are some sources of information you might check out.

1. TAX ASSESSOR'S OFFICE

The City or County Tax Assessor estimates the value of each piece of property and keeps a record of to whom the tax bill is sent and who pays the taxes. This information is kept according to address, so you can obtain it without first knowing he name of the owner.

This can help you identify the real owner. Usually he is the one who pays the taxes. If not, then investigating the person who does pay the tax can lead you to the real owner.

If taxes have not been paid, this indicates either the landlord's poor financial condition or possibly his intent to abandon the building to the city or county.

The amount of the tax is a significant part of the landlord's expense in running the building. You may want to know this for negotiations.

Some assessors keep an alphabetical list of people who pay property taxes, specifying each piece of property on which they pay taxes. This can tell you how much property the landlord owns in the city or county and where it is. If he has other rental buildings, talk to the tenants there and see if they are interested in joining your effort. This can really help you increase the pressure on the landlord.

2. LOCAL REAL ESTATE OFFICES

For income tax reasons, many buildings are put up for sale rather frequently, usually six to ten years after purchase. There is a fair chance that, at any given time, your building will be on the market.

You might send some substantial-looking person into a local real estate office to ask if the building is for sale and express interest in buying it. The real estate agent might furnish him some very helpful information concerning the building, especially information relating to income and expenses. While this information may be slanted to make the building seem more profitable than it is, this bias should make the figures useful to rebut the landlord's inevitable complaints that he is suffering financially from the building.

3. HOUSING CODE INSPECTION DEPARTMENTS

The city or county housing or building inspection department can be a source of information as to the condition of the building and the landlord's efforts (or lack of them) to repair.

First, since he must obtain a permit to make alterations in the building, you can find out when he last made substantial repairs and what he planned to do.

Second, find out when the agency last inspected the building and whether the violations were corrected. This documentation can be useful later for publicity or in court.

Also, find out if they have recorded any complaints by tenants. This can build your case that the tenants have long been concerned about the landlord's failure to repair and are not just creating this issue.

Records of the building inspector's dealings with the landlord are open to the public and may be copied. Government Code Sections 6253 and 7254.7(c).

4. OTHER SOURCES OF INFORMATION

If you want to do a thorough job, here are some other sources of information you might check out.

a. County Recorder's Office
Here, if you know the name of the present owner, you can find out names of prior owners and who has mortgages, deeds of trust, or liens on the property.

b. Title Insurance Companies
They can tell you everything about the ownership of the property, including mortgages, etc. They usually charge for their services, but some people (such as attorneys who do real estate work) can often get information from title companies for nothing.

c. Secretary of State
If the building is owned by a corporation, they will tell you who runs the corporation. Contact the California Secretary of State's Office, 111 Capitol Mall, Sacramento, California 95814.

d. County Tax Assessor's Office
Here you can find out the amount of property taxes your landlord must pay. All you really need to start with is the address of your building. The Assessor's Office can tell you the rest. In many counties, they will give you the information by phone. Also, if you are having trouble finding out who owns your building, the Assessor's Office might help, since they list the person to whom the tax bill is sent.

e. Newspapers
A look through the local newspaper's "morgue" can sometimes produce good information on a landlord. A reporter who has covered the neighborhood for some time might also be helpful.

f. Ex-Managers and Former Tenants

These people may tell you how the landlord has treated people in the past. Since they are out, they have nothing to lose, and if they were mistreated by the landlord, they may be willing to help.

D. TACTICS

1. PETITION THE LANDLORD

The first thing you might do is draw up a petition which sets out your complaints and demands and give it to the landlord.

The petition should be worded politely but firmly. Remember that it might later get into the hands of other people, such as the newspapers or the courts, so you want to sound reasonable, even if the landlord deserves something stronger.

The demands should be clearly set out, and there should be a final demand for a response or a meeting by a specific time (such as a week later). Although it is probably not wise to set out at this point exactly what you intend to do if he is not cooperative (since you want to leave your options open until you are ready to act), the petition should carry the clear implication that the group means business.

It is usually better if all the tenants in the group sign the petition. This lets the landlord know that the people are united and serious enough about this to sign their names and risk possible reprisals. It also tends to make the people feel more committed.

The petition is a useful starting tactic, no matter what else you later decide to do. It forces the group to stop talking about general problems and decide what issues it will focus on. Often it will scare the landlord into submitting to some or all demands. Even if it doesn't, the landlord's response will give you an idea of how to deal with him in the future. Also, if you petition, you can later tell the newspapers, courts, and other groups that you tried to talk to him before you had to resort to your pressure tactics.

2. CALL THE CODE INSPECTOR

Calling the code inspectors and asking for an inspection of the building can be useful for several purposes.

First, an inspection which results in a report that there are violations shows that the tenants have legitimate grievances and are not just making things up to cause trouble or withhold rent. This can help gain public support and impress the courts.

Second, if you end up in court, you have the inspector available as a neutral, expert witness who can testify as to conditions in the building.

Third, an inspection which results in an order from the agency that the landlord make repairs may get him to fix the place, for otherwise the agency might have it condemned. Many sophisticated landlords, however, know how to handle the agency so as to avoid making repairs until the last possible moment. They are friendly with the inspectors, know how to take appeals and get extensions, and perhaps will get the agency to hold off by doing a few things and saying he is "working on" the others. He is less likely to get away with this where there are serious health hazards, such as rats or no heat. If you have these problems, call the Health Department rather than the Building Inspection Department, as they are generally more concerned about these issues.

There are some dangers in reporting code violations. First, if the building is really in bad shape, you may get too much action. The agency may condemn the building, or the landlord may decide it is cheaper to tear it down than fix it up. In either case, the tenants may be evicted.

Second, before calling the inspector, make sure that bad conditions were not caused by tenants, even in part. If they were, the inspector will probably find out about it. In that case, his report will usually do you more harm than good.

Finally, there is a danger of retaliatory eviction if the landlord finds out who reported the violations.* Such evictions are prohibited by law,** and your lawyer should be able to protect you if the landlord tries this.

---

*In some cases, reporting code violations provides protection for subsequent organizing activities since a later eviction will be inferred to be retaliatory.
See Chapter 8; Civil Code Section 1942.5; Moskovitz, **Retaliatory Eviction— A New Doctrine in California, 46 California State Bar Journal 23 (1974).

Before you call out a code inspector, try to find out if there is some inspector in the agency who will be sympathetic to what you are trying to accomplish. If there is, talk to him about these problems and see what he advises. He may be able to set things up so you get the most out of the inspection with the least risk.

3. PICKETING AND PUBLICITY

Landlords don't like negative publicity, particularly if it affects their business or social lives. So it can be a very useful tactic to let the world know that your landlord owns units with serious health or safety problems.

Whenever you seek publicity by any means, make sure that you make specific charges and that what you are saying is true. This will keep you out of legal trouble and keep support on your side.

There are many ways to get publicity. Here are some of them.

Picketing at the building itself involves no travel time or expense, so it is easier to get tenants out to picket. This lets tenants, prospective tenants, and the neighborhood in general know what is going on, and it can help muster support. Picketing at the landlord's office can put economic pressure on him by persuading his customers to stay away. This can be particularly effective when he is a rental agent or management company. A third possible location is the landlord's residence. This can be particularly effective if the landlord lives in an all white suburban neighborhood and the tenants are black or other minority.

Whenever you picket, be sure to contact the newspapers and television stations ahead of time. Their coverage will multiply the effect of your picketing.

Banners in the windows of tenants' apartments are another good way of letting tenants, prospective tenants, and the neighborhood know what is happening. Leaflets can also serve this purpose, and they are good to use when picketing, so people passing by (including reporters) can get the details of the dispute.

A press conference can be a good way of getting into all of the media at once. To get reporters and T.V. people to come, however, you will have to set it up at a time when they can come (that is, when nothing else of importance is happening) and call them personally, well ahead of time. Also, try to make the dispute sound dramatic. If conditions in the building are bad, have the press conference at the building and show the reporters the worst conditions.

If picketing or other publicity is hurting the landlord, he might file a law suit to try to stop it. He may ask the court to limit the number of pickets, stop distribution of material he claims is untrue, or stop the campaign entirely. The law on these issues is not clear, and what happens depends a lot on how the judge feels about it. Therefore, it is very helpful to have a lawyer to advise you and ready to represent you when you start a publicity campaign.

4. RENT STRIKES

The rent strike can be the most powerful tactic the tenants can use. It brings direct and immediate economic pressure to bear on the landlord. Few landlords are able to pay mortgage payments, property taxes, and other expenses from sources other than rents for long. If the landlord cannot break the rent strike quickly, he must come to the bargaining table.

Under a California court decision,* **a rent strike is now legal in California, if** (1) the landlord has materially breached his "implied warranty of habitability" by failing to correct serious housing code violations, (2) tenants did not cause the violations, (3) the landlord was given notice of the violations and a reasonable time to correct them. How these requirements work and what happens if the landlord sues to evict rent strikers is more fully discussed in the section on rent withholding in Chapter 2.

If you decide to rent strike, there are some things you might do to minimize the danger of eviction.

First, line up a good lawyer. If he fights the eviction action very hard and takes advantage of the rights you have,** it may take the

---

*Green v. Superior Court, 10 Cal. 3d 616 (1974)

**Have your lawyer see Moskovitz, Honigsberg and Finkelstein, California Eviction Defense Manual (Cont. Ed. Bar, 1971,) and the Tenant Union Guide for Legal Services Attorneys, in Volume II of the Handbook in Housing Law (Prentice Hall, 1969).

landlord a long time to evict anyone, if he ever can. He might not be able to wait that long, so he may be willing to negotiate.

Second, inform the landlord that you are not simply pocketing the rent money, but are putting it in an "escrow account" which will be disposed of after the dispute is settled (by using it to make repairs, turning it over to the landlord or something else). This escrow account is **not** required by law. But it may impress the judge that you are not just trying to get something for nothing, so he may rule in your favor, or he may at least give you a chance to pay the rent to avoid eviction if he finds that the landlord did not materially breach his implied warranty of habitability. Also, if you dangle a large escrow account in front of a landlord, he will be more willing to deal with you than if the money is simply lost.

An escrow account can be set up as a bank savings account. Everyone deposits his rent in the account. For withdrawals, the signatures of both a tenant organization officer and the tenant should be required. This assures each tenant that his money will not be spent without his consent. An easier way to set up an escrow is to rent a safe deposit box in a bank and have each tenant put a money order (or certified check) for the amount of the rent in the box as it comes due.

Whichever method you choose, make sure that every tenant follows it. If some tenants get a "free ride," morale will suffer badly and the group may easily fall apart.

Third, be sure to put together good evidence on the housing code violations. Take pictures (in color), get a housing code inspector or other expert to look at the place and have tenants ready to testify as to the conditions.

Finally, keep up your campaign for publicity and community support. This can help impress the judge that this is a very important issue.

5. REPAIR AND DEDUCT REMEDY

Another more modest form of rent strike may be permitted in California. The "repair and deduct" remedy, described in detail in Chapter 7, might be used by a group of tenants to make repairs costing no more than the total of the monthly rents of the tenants participating. For example, if the plumbing doesn't work and it will cost $800 to fix, eight tenants might notify the landlord that they will pool their next month's rent of $100 each and have it fixed if he does not do so within a reasonable time. If he fails to do so, the tenants can have the work done, pay the bill, and deduct the amount from the next month's rent. There is presently no reported case in California where tenants have pooled their rents like this, but there seems to be nothing in Civil Code Sections 1941-1942.1 to prevent this.

Many times the threat of using this remedy will itself produce action.

6. LAW SUITS AGAINST THE LANDLORD

A law suit against the landlord can be another means of putting pressure on him so that he wants to negotiate with you. This might be done where he has locked someone out,* committed a retaliatory eviction or rent raise,** or refused to repair substantial housing code violations.***

A law suit puts the landlord on the defensive psychologically. He is in danger of having to pay substantial money damages. He will have to pay attorney's fees, which may be expensive.

If your law suit asks for "punitive damages," your attorney is entitled to find out the landlord's entire financial position, which he may not be anxious to reveal. Your attorney may also take the landlord's "deposition," requiring him to appear and answer questions which might make him uncomfortable.

You should be very careful about the effect on the tenant union of filing such a suit, however. Often when such a suit is filed, the tenants begin to rely too much on the law suit and the lawyer to solve their problems for them. They tend to stop their other efforts and the group gradually fades away. If this happens, even a victory in the law suit usually won't help the tenants much, since most of the tenants will probably move out before then. Be sure to tell the

---

*Jordan v. Talbot, 55 Cal 2d 597; 12 Cal. Rptr. 488 (1961).
**Aweeka v. Bonds, 20 Cal. App. 3d 278 (1971); Civil code Section 1942.5.
  But see Newby v. Alto Riviera Apts., 131 Cal. Rptr. 547 (1976).
***Quevedo v. Braga, 72 Cal. App. 3d Supp. 1 (1977); Stoiber v. Honeychuck, 162 Cal. Rptr, 194 (1980).

people (and the attorney) that the law suit is only one part of the campaign against the landlord to force him to negotiate with the tenant union. If they cannot accept this, then you probably should not file the suit.

7. LANDLORD'S COUNTERTACTICS

There are several things the landlord is likely to try to defeat your movement. He might file law suits against the tenants or try to get the police to stop the picketing. He might try to evict the leaders of the tenant union, or, thinking that if just one person is evicted the tenant union will collapse, he may try to evict one person he has good legal grounds to evict. He may try to pit certain tenants against others, making promises to some and blaming problems on others. A common tactic is to surprise the tenants by giving in to most of their demands right away with promises, then waiting for the group to fade away and then doing little or nothing.

The tenants should be aware of these possibilities and be ready to deal with them. They should remember to (1) always stick together and (2) don't relax until they have the final action they seek.

E. NEGOTIATIONS

Skill in negotiating is very important to maximize the results of your campaign against the landlord. Never forget, however, that the outcome will depend much more on who has the power outside the negotiating room, that is, what you can do to the landlord if he won't give you what you want and what you can give him if he will. The most skillful negotiator can't do much for powerless people, but inarticulate amateurs can often succeed when their opponent understands that they can and will use some real power if he does not give in.

1. PREPARATIONS

The tenant union should select a small negotiating team to speak for them.

These people should know as much as possible about the building, the tenants and the landlord. Psychologically, the landlord can gain control of the negotiating meeting if he overwhelms the tenants with his knowledge, so the tenants had better be prepared to keep up with him.

The negotiators should have a clear understanding of what their authority is, that is, what kind of deal the tenants will accept. The tenants should discuss their demands and tell the negotiators which demands are non-negotiable, which are "nice if they can get it," and which are expendable and can be traded off. In deciding this, the tenants must understand how strong they are and what they can realistically expect to get.

A role-playing session, with some tenants playing the landlord's role, can be very helpful to give the negotiators some experience.

The negotiators should have a proposed collective bargaining agreement ready at the meeting, so that they can get the landlord to commit himself in writing then and there. If there is nothing for him to sign, he might promise to sign something but change his mind later.

Finally, the negotiators should put together an overall strategy, knowing what they are after and how they are going to get there, so they can work together and not interfere with each other.

2. THE NEGOTIATING MEETING

The meeting should not take place at the landlord's office, where he will feel comfortable and the tenants intimidated. Have the meeting at the building or somewhere else in your neighborhood.

Have as many tenants as possible attend the meeting. This show of unity will impress the landlord and help the negotiators. It will also stimulate tenant interest and help strengthen the tenant union.

Make sure that the person you negotiate with is the owner or has the authority to make decisions binding on the owner. If this isn't made clear at the outset, they are wasting your time.

The negotiators should get across to the landlord—directly or subtly—what the union will do if negotiations break down and what they will give him if he comes to terms. On this latter point, you might tell the landlord that the tenant union and a collective bargaining agreement giving rights to tenants can increase tenant morale. This can cut down vandalism and vacancies and make rent payments more prompt.

One of the most important elements in negotiations is the psychological atmosphere. The landlord will try to be in control and keep the negotiators on the defensive. The negotiators should realize this and try to keep the landlord on the defensive.

F. THE COLLECTIVE BARGAINING AGREEMENT

The collective bargaining agreement is a key goal of the tenant union. Labor unions seek such agreements in order to firmly establish a continuing bargaining relationship with an employer, as well as to settle specific points of dispute. Tenant union collective bargaining agreements can do the same, so that the landlord has to deal with the union rather than the isolated tenant, and so the tenant can have the power of the union behind him whenever he has a grievance.

Remember, however, that the agreement will only be as effective as the continued willingness of the tenant union to make it effective. Even though the agreement is legally binding on the landlord, experience has shown that it will simply fade away unless the tenant union (or some larger neighborhood organization) is continually around as a "watchdog" to see that the landlord complies with it.

Here is a brief form* of collective bargaining agreement you may want to have adapted to fit your particular situation. Tell your lawyer what you want so he can write it in language that will be legally binding.

Take a copy of the signed and notarized agreement to the County Recorder's Office to have it recorded. This may prevent someone who buys the building from trying to avoid the agreement.

---

*A more extensive model agreement, with explanatory notes, appears in the **Tenant Union Guide**, in Volume II of the **Handbook on Housing Law** (Prentice-Hall, 1969).

COLLECTIVE BARGAINING AGREEMENT

I

Parties

The parties to this Agreement are _____ ,
hereinafter called "Landlord," and _____ ,
hereinafter called "Union."* The property covered by this
Agreement is located at _____ .

II

Purpose

It is the general purpose of this agreement to provide a
better means of communication between Landlord and his
tenants, through Union, their bargaining agent, to assure a
continuous harmonious relationship and an orderly method
of resolving differences and grievances, which will result in a
stable tenancy, reduced expenses through greater tenant
concern, and a better community.

III

Dismissal of Pending Lawsuits

All lawsuits currently pending between Landlord and
Union or Landlord and any member of Union shall be
dismissed, including the following: _____
_____ .

---

*Many groups will want to use the word "organization" rather than "union." Suit
yourself, it makes no legal difference.

IV

Recognition of Union

Landlord recognizes Union as the sole collective bargaining agent for its members who are tenants at the property covered by this Agreement on all matters relating to their tenancies, the building, and their dealings with Landlord in his capacity as owner.

V

Union Security

Landlord shall in no way discriminate against or take reprisals against any person because of his involvement or sympathy with Union. Nor shall Landlord promise or give any benefits to any peron conditioned on such person's quitting, failing to join, or refusing to assist Union in any way.

VI

Tenant Responsibilities

Union agrees and recognizes that each tenant has certain obligations and responsibilities, including the following, and Union agrees to take no action to discourage tenants from complying with these obligations and responsibilities:

1. To pay rent promptly when due (except where provided other wise by law, this Agreement, or agreement between Landlord and a tenant);

2. To pay for and correct any damage to the premises or Landlord's furnishings caused by any intentional or negligent act of a tenant or any person occupying the premises with his permission, excepting damage to normal wear and tear;

3. To place his garbage and refuse inside the containers provided therefor;

4. To refrain from acts which unduly disturb his neighbors;

5. To obey all state and local laws and regulations relating to the occupancy of residential property;

6. To comply with his obligations under his lease or rental agreement.

VII

Leases [or Rental Agreements]

A standard form Model Lease [or Model Rental Agreement]* is attached to this Agreement and labelled "Exhibit A."

Within seven days of this Agreement, Landlord shall offer to sign such Model with each tenant who is a member of Union. Landlord shall make the same offer to each new member of Union within seven days of being notified of such membership by Union.

The provisions of this Agreement shall be considered incorporated into and a part of each such Model signed.

VIII

Rents

1. *Rents.* The following monthly rentals shall apply to the following units:

Apartment number
(specify furnished or unfurnished)   Rent

2. *Appliances.* Landlord shall, without extra charge, furnish every apartment with a satisfactory stove and refrigerator, which he shall maintain in good working order.

3. *Utilities.* Landlord shall provide and pay for the following utilities, without adding to the monthly rent: gas, electricity,

---

*See APPENDIX for a Model to use.

water, garbage collection, trash removal and sewer charges.

4. *Late Charges.* No late charges or fines shall be imposed.

5. *Rent Increases.* There shall be no rent increases during the term of this agreement.

6. *Back Rents.* Back rents in the amount of _____ now held by Union shall be disposed of as follows: _____

_____.

IX

Repairs and Maintenance

1. *Maintenance.* Landlord shall maintain the building and grounds in a decent, safe and sanitary condition, and shall comply with all state and local laws, regulations and ordinances concerning the maintenance of residential property. In addition, as specific maintenance problems have arisen in the past, Landlord specifically agrees to provide the following maintenance services:

[*Example:* (a) check the coin-operated washing machine and dryer at least once a week to see that they are in good operating condition;

(b) repair broken mailboxes upon notice by affected tenants.]

2. *Security.* Landlord shall take reasonable measures to maintain security in the building and grounds to protect the tenants and their guests from burglary, robbery and other crimes.

3. *Repairs.* Landlord shall complete the following repairs by the following dates:

Repair	Date

4. *Failure to Comply.* Union shall have the right to inspect the building at reasonable times to insure compliance with this Section. If any repair is not completed by the date specified, or if Landlord fails to comply with any maintenance duty for seven days or longer, the tenants of the building may thereafter, until completion of repairs or resumption of maintenance, pay their rent into a bank account held by Union. Union shall use the money to make the repairs or perform the maintenance, remitting the balance to Landlord after repairs are completed and maintenance resumed. This remedy shall be in addition to any remedies provided by law or contract for tenants receiving inadequate maintenance or repair.

X

Grievance Procedure

1. The term "grievance" shall mean any dispute between Landlord and a tenant or between Landlord and Union involving the interpretation, application, or coverage of this Agreement or any lease or rental agreement, except that any claim for personal injuries exceeding $500 shall not be considered a "grievance" subject to this procedure.

2. Any tenant having a grievance may present his grievance, by himself or through Union, to Landlord or his agent.

3. If the grievance has not been resolved to the satisfactin of the tenant within ten days after being presented, a grievance meeting shall be held between the tenant, Union, and Landlord within the next five days, or as soon thereafter as the parties may agree. At such meeting, the parties shall attempt to resolve the grievance to everyone's satisfaction.

4. If Landlord has a grievance against any tenant, or against Union, he may present such grievance to Union, which shall attempt to resolve the grievance as soon as possible.

5. If Landlord's grievance has not been resolved to his satisfaction within ten days after it has been presented to Union, the grievance meeting provisions subsection 3 above shall apply.

6. If the grievance meeting produces no resolution of the grievance, the aggrieved party may then file suit in any court of competent jurisdiction for final determination of the matter in dispute.*

XI

Enforcement

The provisions of this Agreement may be enforced through appropriate legal action by Landlord, Union, or any affected person. As the amount of damages attributable to violation of any provision of this Agreement may be difficult to ascertain, the parties agree that these provisions may be specifically enforced by an appropriate court.

XII

Severability

In the event that any provision of this Agreement is deemed invalid by any court of law, it is mutually agreed that such determination shall not affect any other provisions of this Agreement and the Agreement shall remain binding on all parties hereto.

XIII

Union's Right to Information

In order to enable Union to maintain a continuing interest in the present and future condition of the building and to adequately represent the interests of the tenants, Landlord

---

*For a grievance procedure containing a provision for arbitration by a neutral arbitrator before going to court, see the **Tenant Union Guide**, in Volume II of the **Handbook on Housing Law** (Prentice-Hall, 1969).

shall furnish Union with information and allow Union to examine Landlord's records and books, upon reasonable notice by Union, relating to the following matters:

1. expenses of maintaining the building;

2. income received from the building;

3. all other financial information relating to the building, including mortgages or deeds of trust on the building, and

4. all taxes affected by the building.

XIV

Duration

This Agreement shall remain in full force and effect from the date it is signed by both Landlord and Union and until _____ 19__.

On _____ 19__, Landlord and Union shall begin negotiations for a new agreement to go into effect at the expiration of this Agreement. Such negotiations shall continue in good faith until a new agreement is reached or this Agreement expires.

WHEREFORE, We, the undersigned, do hereby execute and agree to this Agreement.

For the Landlord:

1. _____
   (signature)

_____
   (title)

_____
   (date of signature)

2. _____
   (signature)

_____
   (title)

_____
   (date of signature)

For the Union:

1. _____
   (signature)

_____
   (title)

_____
   (date of signature)

2 _____
   (signature)

_____
   (title)

_____
   (date of signature)

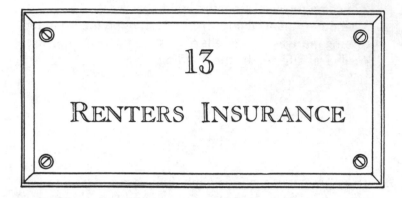

13
RENTERS INSURANCE

Attitudes toward insurance vary—some people wouldn't be without it while others consider it a giant rip-off. Our job is not to argue this question one way or the other, but to tell you how renters insurance works.

Renters insurance is a package of several types of insurance designed to cover tenants from more than one risk. Different insurance companies put slightly different things in their packages, both as to types of coverage, dollar amounts of coverage and especially deductible clauses. There is nothing we can tell you here that will substitute for your shopping around and comparing policies and prices. They do vary. It's a good idea to talk to friends and see if they are happy with their insurance, but realize that prices for renters insurance can be very different depending upon where you live. In certain high theft areas it is almost unattainable.

The average renters policy covers you against losses to your belongings occurring as a result of fire and theft up to the amount stated on the face of the policy which is often $5,000, $10,000 or $25,000. As thefts have become more common, most policies have included "deductible" amounts of $50, $100, or even $500. This means that if you are burgled, you collect from the insurance company only for the amount of your loss over and above the "deductible" clause.

184

Many renters policies completely exclude certain property from theft coverage, including cash, credit cards, pets, etc., while others limit the amount of cash covered to $100, the value of manuscripts to $1,000 and jewelry and furs to $500. Make sure your policy covers what you think it does. If it doesn't, check out the policies of other companies. As a general rule you can get whatever coverage you want if you are willing to pay for it.

If you do take out insurance on valuable items, you should inventory them. Not only should you note them down with their values, it is also an excellent idea to take photos. Keep the inventory and the photos *out* of your apartment.

In addition to fire and theft coverage most renters policies give you, and your family living with you, personal liability coverage to a certain amount stated in the policy. This means that if you directly injure someone (you hit them on the head with a golf ball), they are injured on the rental property that you occupy through your negligence (they slip on a broken front step), or you damage their belongings (your garden hose floods the neighbor's cactus garden), you are covered. There are a lot of exclusions to personal liability coverage, important among them being any damage you do with a motor vehicle, boat or through your business.

IMPORTANT: Your landlord's "homeowners" insurance won't cover you. Even if you live in a duplex with your landlord and the landlord has a "homeowners" policy, this policy won't protect your belongings if there is a fire or theft. Of course, if you suffer a loss as a result of your landlord's negligence, you may have a valid claim against him. Some large landlords have insurance to specifically protect against this sort of risk.

If you have a loss, be sure your insurance company treats you fairly. You are entitled to the present fair market value (not the replacement cost) of anything stolen or detroyed by fire or any other hazard covered by the policy after the deductible amount of the policy is subtracted. If the company won't pay you a fair amount, consider taking the dispute to Small Claims Court if it is $1500 or less. If the loss is a major one, you might consider seeing a lawyer, but agree to pay the lawyer only a percentage of what he or she can recover over and above what the insurance company offers you without the lawyer's help.

Note: Many landlords insert a clause into their lease or rental agreement requiring that the tenant purchase renter's insurance. This is legal under California law. The landlord's motive for doing so is threefold:

1. If the property is damaged in any way and the damage is covered by the renter's policy, the landlord won't have to rely on his own insurance policy;

2. Anyone who suffers a personal injury on the property in a situation where the tenant is liable is less likely to also sue the landlord;

3. A number of landlords believe that tenants who are willing to buy insurance are more responsible than other tenants.

14
CONDOMINIUM
CONVERSION

Converting buildings from rental properties to condominiums was unusual several years ago. Now, however, the general shortage of new homes, coupled with favorable tax laws, has created a condominium boom.

Condominium ownership as an abstract principle can make great sense. People have a basic need to own their own spaces, and with the high cost of land and construction, condominiums are often the only way this need can find expression. But whether condominium ownership makes sense as an abstract principle need not concern us here—there are already more than enough people worrying about how to create more of them while getting paid plenty for their efforts. Our concern is with the tenants of existing rental properties who are unable or unwilling to pay large sums of money to purchase their units.

One day the mailperson delivers an identical letter to all the tenants in a multi-unit building. The owner, it seems, has decided to convert the building from rental units to an owner-occupied condominium. Everyone will have to either buy his or her apartment and a share of the common space such as halls and grounds, or move out. Those with leases must leave when they run out, and those with month-to-month tenancies under a written rental agreement must leave in thirty days. The letter concludes politely that the owners hope that they have caused no inconvenience and are sure that many tenants will welcome this opportunity to buy their units at the rock bottom price of $100,000 each.

Is there anything a tenant can do in the above situation if he wants neither to move nor buy his unit? Can't the landlord do pretty much what he or she wants? At first impression it would seem that the law favors the landlord and that the tenant is in a hopeless position, but don't give up too fast. Some very determined tenants in many cities have proved that tenants acting together aren't helpless.

The conversion of rental units to a condominium constitutes a subdivision under California law. This means that several local government agencies have the right to approve or disapprove the project. A public hearing must be held before the planning commission, with an appeal to the city council or county board of supervisors. Tenants acting together have stopped many conversions by exerting sufficient political pressure so that proposed conversions were denied the necessary approvals. One of the best ways to do this is to have the local government involved pass an ordinance allowing condominium conversion only if a number of conditions have been met. Your city or county may already have passed such an ordinance, and your first step is to get a copy if one exists. But beware, many ordinances purporting to strictly limit condominium conversions were, in fact, written by developers and have no real teeth.

A good condominium conversion ordinance should require most, if not all, of the following conditions to be met, before a conversion can take place:
- That existing tenants be given first right to buy their unit;
- That 50% of the existing tenants approve of the conversion;
- That all tenants over 65 or disabled be allowed to continue as tenants for life if they wish;
- That no conversions be allowed where the landlord has evicted large groups of tenants or greatly raised rents to get rid of tenants just prior to the conversion;
- That no conversions of any kind be allowed when the rental vacancy rate in a city is below 5% unless new rental units are being built at least fast enough to replace those converted;
- That special scrutiny be given to conversion of units rented to

people with low and moderate incomes to see that they are priced at a level that the existing tenants can afford;

● That the landlord provide **adequate** relocation assistance.

To have a chance to stop a proposed condominium conversion, it is essential that tenants act together and that they create political alliances with sympathetic groups in the city. If you have not already done so, read Chapter 11. You will want to start by checking out your landlord carefully. Look for facts about the landlord that would tend to make local government agencies unsympathetic to the conversion. Among the best are the following:

● The landlord is from out of town and has recently bought your building (and perhaps) others as a speculation;

● The landlord has a long history of violating housing codes and generally is known as a "bad landlord";

● The landlord raised rents excessively, terminated tenancies for no reason, and did other things to clear out the building before the conversion was announced;

● The building is occupied by many older people (or others on fixed incomes) who have no place to go, and the landlord has made little or no effort to either allow them to stay on at terms they can afford or find them a decent place to live;

● The landlord is making an excellent return on his or her money as rental units and conversion to condominiums would result in huge profits.

NOTE: Legislation has recently been introduced in the state legislature to provide strict rules covering condominium conversions. To date, nothing has passed, largely as a result of pressure from the real estate lobby. The only statewide ruling affecting conversions is found in Government Code 66247.1. It provides only that:

1. Each tenant is given 120 days' written notice of the intent to convert prior to termination of tenancy due to the conversion, and

2. Each tenant is given the first right to buy his or her apartment on at least the same terms that the apartment will be offered to the general public. The tenant has 90 days to decide.

So, if you are faced with a condominium conversion, don't give up. Re-read this chapter and get together with your neighbors and organize. You will probably find that the other tenants in your city face similar situations. Together you may be able to exert enough political pressure to save your home.

15

RENT CONTROL

A. LOCAL LAWS

California presently has no statewide rent control law and it is not likely one will be adopted in the near future, due to the lobbying power of landlord and real estate groups. It is possible to establish rent control on a local basis, either through the initiative process or by the act of a city council or a county board of superivsors.* Some cities and counties have enacted local ordinances which do limit the rents landlords can charge, as well as instituting other protections beneficial to tenants.

Rent control got a big boost in California in 1978 as a result of political fallout after Proposition 13 was enacted. Even though Proposition 13 reduced landlords' property taxes as much as two-thirds, many, if not most, landlords refused to share any of these savings with their tenants who, in many cases, had had their rents raised repeatedly in previous years because taxes had gone up. Some landlords even increased rents. To make matters worse, rampant real estate speculation resulted in rapidly accelerating real estate prices and new rental property owners commonly

---

*The California Supreme Court upheld the right of cities to enact rent control ordinances in **Birkenfeld v. City of Berkeley**, 17 Cal. 3d 129. (1976).

passed these increased costs on to their tenants. High profit condominium conversions also became common and resulted in reducing the supply of rental housing and thus driving up the price of what was left.

Many tenants have refused to accept large rent increases and have organized locally to see that rent gouging is stopped. As a result, some form of rent regulation now exists in a number of California communities, including Los Angeles, San Jose, and San Francisco (see chart below). Before we describe how such regulation works, a few words of caution:

- Rent control is a rapidly changing field. Hardly a month goes by without one or another city or county changing (or adopting) an ordinance. In addition, many ordinances automatically expire after a certain period of time. Finally, various rent control provisions are presently being challenged in court. In short, you should read the material here only to get a general idea of the field. It is absolutely necessary that you also contact your city or county to find out whether rent control exists, and if it does, to get a copy of the ordinance and any regulations interpreting it.

- No two rent control ordinances are exactly alike. Some cities have elected or appointed boards which have the power to adjust rents; others allow a certain percentage increase each year as part of their ordinances. Some cities have enlightened ordinances with "just cause" for eviction provisions which require landlords to give and prove valid reasons for terminating month-to-month tenancies while other cities in effect encourage landlords to evict by allowing unlimited rent increases on units when they are vacated. In order to summarize how each ordinance works, we have prepared a "Rent Regulation" chart which outlines the major points of each ordinance. We don't have the space to develop the details of all the various ordinances, so again it will be up to you to contact your city or county clerk to get a copy of the entire ordinance in your area;

- The California Housing Research Foundation publishes "CHAIN Letter" to keep tenants advised of rent regulation laws as they are passed or amended. Their address is P.O. Box 20226, Oakland, CA 94620.

B. HOW THE "RENT REGULATION" CHART WORKS

The Rent Regulation Chart in this chapter briefly summarizes the major features of various cities' rent control ordinances under the following headings:

Locality: Most rent control ordinances are adopted by cities, and so apply throughout a particular city. But watch it if you live in Los Angeles **County.** The County has adopted rent control, but it applies only in "unincorporated areas," not in cities which happen to lie inside the county. Several of these, such as Los Angeles, Beverly Hills and Santa Monica have adopted their own different ordinances.

Exemptions: Ordinances don't cover all rental housing within the "locality." Commonly, owner occupied buildings with four (or sometimes three) units or less and new construction are exempted from rent control ordinances. Some cities also exempt luxury units, single family dwellings, etc.

Registration: Some cities having rent control require the owners of units subject to control to register their units with the agency which administers the rent control ordinance. This allows the agency to keep track of the city's rental units and obtain operating funds from the registration fees. Berkeley and Santa Monica allow tenants to withhold rent payments if a landlord fails to register. Other cities require no registration at all.

Administration: Most rent control ordinances are administered by a rent control board whose members are appointed (elected in Santa Monica) by the mayor, city council, or board of supervisors. The formal name, address and phone number of the board is given.

Rent Formula and Individual Adjustments: In this column you will find a brief summary of the mechanism each city follows to allow rent increases. Most cities have two principal ways of doing this. First, general percentage increases are allowed periodically, either by action of the board (as in Santa Monica and Berkeley) or by allowing specified increases over given time periods (in San Francisco, San Jose, and Los Angeles). Second, in most cities, landlords (and sometimes tenants) may petition the board for a higher (or lower) rent level based on certain criteria, such as recovering the costs of improvements, increased finance costs, etc.

Vacancy Decontrol: Some cities apply rent control only for as long as a tenant continues to live in the same place. If that tenant leaves, the landlord can charge any rent he or she wants when the unit is re-rented. This is called "vacancy decontrol," and it is a bad feature. It means tenants get hurt badly when they have to move to another unit in the city. It also means that city-wide rents tend to rise almost as much as they do without rent control (since most tenants move every few years). And finally, it has the nasty side-effect of encouraging landlords to make tenants so miserable that they will "voluntarily" leave, or even to evict them outright with a 30-day notice.

Eviction Protection: If a city has "vacancy decontrol," as many rent control ordinances do, it is almost essential that the ordinance also require that a tenant can be evicted only for "just cause," and not simply because the landlord wants him out. Under most ordinances "just cause" for eviction includes not paying the legal rent, disturbing other tenants, damaging the premises, breaking th rental agreement, violating reasonable rules, etc. Without a "just cause" provision, an epidemic of evictions is almost sure to occur. Under this heading you will learn whether your city has an "eviction protection" provision. A few cities that have no such protection forbid "retaliatory eviction," where the landlord gives the tenant a 30-day Notice to Quit in order to retaliate against the tenant's exercise of his or her rights under the rent control law (i.e., by insisting on not paying any more than the legal rent, or by objecting to an illegal rent increase). Unfortunately, under this sort of ordinance, the tenant has to prove, in court (which usually means hiring a lawyer), that the landlord's reason for eviction was retaliatory in nature, which is difficult to do.

C. FIGHT BACK AGAINST CHEATING LANDLORDS

In all cities with rent control, some landlords have cheated—

that is, have raised rents more than the allowed amount or have otherwise violated rent control provisions. We simply don't have space to list all landlord tricks, but here are several of the most common: *

- **The Phony Relative Caper:** Under rent control ordinances that have a provision calling for "just cause" for eviction, one allowable reason to evict a tenant is because the landlord or a close relative wants to live in the unit. Many times landlords have invoked this provision to move a tenant out, only to have the relative disappear entirely or only live in a unit for a month or two. If you are threatened with eviction for this reason, satisfy yourself that the relative is real and is honestly going to live in the unit. If there are **other vacant** apartments in the building into which the landlord could move his relative, his attempt to evict you is probably an attempt to free another apartment for higher rent under "vacancy decontrol." If you suspect fraud, howl to your local rent control board and/or investigate the possibility of legal action. In San Francisco, for example, you can recover certain statutory punitive damages if a landlord can be shown to have employed a trick to get around the ordinance. *

- **The Phony Repair Gambit:** Another legitimate "just cause" for eviction involves the landlord claiming that he plans major repairs. Here again, once the tenant has moved out, repairs aren't always made. If you suspect fraud, check to see if the landlord has taken out a building permit. If he hasn't, don't move. Also, you may want to suggest that you will let the landlord do the repairs one room at a time while you live in the others. *

- **The "Coerced Consent" Ploy:** Many tenants have their rent raised too much simply because they let the landlord get away with it. This can occur because the landlord threatens to make the tenant's life miserable, to evict the tenant, or in some other way to make the tenant suffer unless the tenants go along with a large increase. If this happens to you, complain. (See D, below.)

- **The Landlord is an Ogre Act:** Especially in cities where a landlord can raise rents when a tenant voluntarily leaves, some landlords have simply set out to make a tenant miserable enough to move. This can involve violations of privacy, poor

---

*For example, a San Francisco tenant recently won a $10,000 award, which was then tripled to $30,000 under the local ordinance, from a landlord who evicted him. The landlord allegedly planned to occupy the apartment himself, but he occupied it for only one month and then re-rented it for more than twice the original rent.

maintenance, and other harrassment techniques. If you suspect that this is happening to you, document as much of the land-lord's conduct as possible and fight back. (See D, below.)

NOTE: A recent case has held that a tenant is entitled to sue a landlord for bad faith acts that occur after an unlawful detainer judgment has been rendered in favor of the landlord. The tenant was evicted on the grounds the landlord wanted to take the unit off the housing market. The tenant challenged the landlord's good faith (required under the Los Angeles rent control ordinance) but lost a jury verdict. LAter, the landlord leased the premises to others at a higher rent. The tenant sued. The court of appeal ruled that the earlier judgment did not preclude the second suit. This case may be applicable to other rent control areas and essentially gives the tenant recourse for a landlord's actions that occur after an eviction. **Brossard v. Stotter,** Ct. of App. 10/16/84.

D. WHAT TO DO IF THE LANDLORD VIOLATES RENT CONTROL

- Get a copy of your local ordinance—and any regulation interpreting it—and make sure you are right;
- If you think your landlord may have made a good faith mistake, try to work the problems out informally;
- Contact any local tenants rights organization and get the benefit of their advice;
- File a formal complaint with your city rent board;
- If the landlord's conduct is extreme, talk to a lawyer. You may have a valid suit based on the intentional inflictionof emotional distress, for invasion of privacy, or on some other grounds, including those provided in the ordinance itself.

E. RENT "MEDIATION"

In a few cities where city councils have felt tenant pressure, but not enough pressure to enact rent control ordinances, so-called voluntary rent "guidelines," or landlord-tenant "mediation" services have been adopted. The chief beneficiaries of these dubious standards and procedures seem to be the landlords, since voluntary programs have no power and infrequently stop rent increases. On rare occasions, however, voluntary mediation or guidelines may work, particularly with smaller landlords who are trying to be fair. If your city or county isn't on the rent control list, check to see if it has a voluntary program.

BERKELEY*

Exceptions:	New construction; Owner-occupied two units or less; Transients.
Registrations:	Required, or landlord can't raise rents and tenants can withhold current rents. Stiff penalties for non-cooperation.
Administration:	Appointed: Rent Stabilization Board, 2180 Milvia Street, Berkeley, CA 94709, (415) 644-6128.
Rent Formula:	6/3/80 freeze at 5/31/80 levels, plus annual adjustments by Board after investigation and hearings. Rents of units exempt before June 1982 are frozen at 12/31/81 levels.
Individual Adjustments:	Landlord may apply for further increase for unusually high utility or maintenance costs, and tenant is notified of hearing. Tenant may seek rent reduction for poor maintenance.
Vacancy Decontrol:	No.
Eviction Protection:	Very strict just-cause eviction provisions; retaliation prohibited.
Other Features:	Landlords who fail to make city-ordered repairs can't raise rent.

BEVERLY HILLS

Exceptions:	New construction; Units renting for over $600/month when ordinance was adopted.
Registrations:	No.
Administration:	Appointed 7-member Rent Adjustments Board, City Manager's Office, 450 N. Crescent Drive, Beverly Hills, CA, (213) 550-4939.
Rent Formula:	Annual increases limited to 8% or the annual Consumer Price Index increase; whichever is less. In addition, an additional increase of up to 4% is allowed when the landlord "amortizes" (spreads out over 5 years or more) the cost of capital improvements.
Individual Adjustments:	Landlords can seek further increases for "undue economic hardship."
Vacancy Decontrol:	Yes, if vacancy is "voluntary."
Eviction Protection:	Just cause eviction; retaliation prohibited.
Other Features:	Landlord must give tenant one year notice of intent to convert unit to condominium, and must pay tenant a relocation allowance of up to $2500, depending on length of tenancy and other factors.

COTATI**

Exceptions:	None (other than government-subsidized units).
Registrations:	Required, or landlord can't raise rents and tenant can seek Board's permission to withhold rent.

---

*As of this writing, the question of whether Berkeley's ordinance is constitutional is pending before the California Supreme Court, which might not rule for a year or two. Until that time, the ordinance is still in effect.

**A recent Court of Appeal case upheld the Cotati rent control ordinance, which bases rents on the amount actually invested in the property by the landlord. The court refused to allow landlords to charge rent based on the current (usually greatly increased) value of the property, because it would lead to rent gouging. COTATI ALLIANCE FOR BETTER HOUSING V. CITY OF COTATI, 148 CA.3d 280 (1983).

Administration:	Appointed 5-member Rent Appeals Board, P.O. Box 428, Cotati, CA 94928, (707) 795-5478.
Rent Formula:	Annual rent increases limited to 66% (two-thirds) of the annual Consumer Price Index increase for residential rents in the San Francisco Bay Area.
Individual Adjustments:	No.
Vacancy Decontrol:	No.
Eviction Protection:	Cotati has a separate ordinance requiring just cause for evictions, and retaliatory eviction is prohibited by the rent control ordinance.

HAYWARD

Exceptions:	New construction; Units owned by landlord owning 4 or less rental units in the city.
Registrations:	No.
Administration:	Administered by Rent Review Office. 22300 Foothill Blvd., Hayward, CA 94541, (415) 581-2345 ext. 214.
Rent Formula:	Annual rent increases limited in any 12-month period to 7% plus increased utility costs. (See warning below.)
Individual Adjustments:	**Warning:** When the landlord increases the rent over 7%, the tenant must file a petition before the increase takes effect (30 days), or will lose the right to object to it. (Landlord may be allowed to pass on increased utility and maintenance costs and "amortized" (spread-out) capital expenditures.) Disputes are heard by a 3-member mediation-arbitration panel. If mediation fails, arbitration is mandatory and binding on both parties.
Vacancy Decontrol:	Allowed if vacancy was voluntary, the landlord spends $200 or more on improvements afterward, and obtains city certification of compliance with building codes.
Eviction Protection:	Hayward requires the landlord to have just cause to evict, even as to units earlier exempted because of vacancy decontrol.

LOS ANGELES (CITY)

Exceptions:	Units constructed since 10/1/78 or "substantially renovated" (with at least $10,000 in improvements) since then; "Luxury" units; single-family houses, unless 3 or more on a lot.
Registrations:	Required, or tenants can withhold rents. **Note:** Once the landlord registers, however, the tenant(s) must pay all the back rent withheld because of the landlord's failure to register, so rent withheld for this reason should be kept in a savings account.
Administration:	Appointed 7-member Rent Adjustment Commission, 215 West 6th Street, Los Angeles, CA 90014, (213) 485-4727.
Rent Formula:	Rents may not be increased more than 7% in any 12-month period without permission of Commission or Community Development Department. However if the landlord pays for utilities for the unit, s/he may raise the rent an additional 1% for each type of utility service.

Individual Adjustments:	Landlord may apply to Rent Adjustment Commission for higher increase to obtain "just and reasonable return" (does not include "negative cash flow" based on recent purchase, but does include negative "operating expenses" not counting the landlord's mortgage payment). Also, landlord may apply to the Community Development Department for permission to pass on to the tenant the cost of capital improvements not directly benefitting the landlord (e.g., new roof but not new swimming pool adding to value) spread out over 5 or more years.
Vacancy Decontrol:	Yes, if tenant vacated voluntarily or was evicted for good cause.
Eviction Protection:	**Warning:** Los Angeles has just-cause eviction and retaliation protections, but also allows vacancy decontrol if tenant "vacated voluntarily" or was evicted for good cause. This encourages landlords to find "reasons" (such as one loud party) to evict tenants in order to escape rent control. This is very bad.

LOS ANGELES COUNTY
(unincorporated area only—not cities)

Exceptions:	Units where tenancy began after 7/22/79; Luxury units; Single family homes.
Registrations:	No.
Administration:	Appointed 15-member Rent Adjustment Commission organized into five 3-member panels. (Call County Rent Control Office at (213) 520-9022.)
Rent Formula:	Rents may not be increased more than 9% in any 12-month period, but utility cost increases can be passed to tenants in addition. Also, the landlord can pass on the amortized cost of assessments imposed by government agencies.
Individual Adjustments:	The landlord may apply to the Commission for additional increases to pay for capital improvements, or if s/he is not obtaining a "just return" on the property.
Vacancy Decontrol:	Yes, if vacancy is "voluntary" or tenant was evicted for nonpayment of rent, or landlord moved in a member of his/her family for at least six months. **Note:** This last reason causes landlords to play all sorts of games to avoid rent control.
Eviction Protection:	Just cause required to evict, but includes landlord moving relative into unit (in order to escape rent control); this is very bad. Retaliatory eviction prohibited.
Other Features:	The current ordinance is due to expire in 1985, on the "anniversary month" coinciding with the month the tenancy began; for example, rent control will end in February 1985 for tenants who moved in during the month of February and so on. (This method of "decontrol" is in addition to ordinary vacancy decontrol.)

LOS GATOS

Exceptions:	Lots with 3 or fewer rental units; Single-family houses. Rented condominium units.
Registrations:	No.

Administration: The Los Gatos Rental Mediation program is located at 3275 Stevens Creek Blvd. #310, San Jose, CA 95117, (408) 395-6350.

Rent Formula: Rents may not be increased by more than 70% of the average annual Consumer Price Index increase in urban San Francisco and Oakland, or 5%, whichever is greater.

Individual Adjustments: **Warning:** Landlords can raise rents as high as they want unless 25% or more of the tenants in the building protest. The tenants call the Rental Mediation Program to start a binding mediation-arbitration process.

Vacancy Decontrol: Yes, if voluntary.

Eviction Protection: There is no just-cause requirement for eviction as such, but a tenant faced with a 30-day termination notice can attempt mediation. If that doesn't work, the tenant can insist on binding arbitration, and the landlord must comply with the arbitrator's decision. Retaliatory evictions are prohibited.

OAKLAND

Exceptions: None; applies to residential rental units.

Registrations: No.

Administration: Appointed 7-member Residential Rent Arbitration Board, 1421 Washington Street, Room 414, Oakland, CA, (415) 273-3371.

Rent Formula: Rents may not be increased more than 8% in any 12-month period after May 6, 1980. An extra 2% increase in such 12-month period is allowed if the unit is vacated.

Individual Adjustments: If landlord raises rent more than amount allowed by rent formula, tenant may seek a hearing within 30 days. Hearing officers decide cases, with the possibility of appeal to the Board.

Vacancy Decontrol: Yes, if voluntary.

Eviction Protection: Retaliatory eviction prohibited; no requirement for just-cause for evictions.

PALM SPRINGS

Exceptions: New construction (April 1979); Owner-occupied 4 units or less; Units where rent exceeded $450/month in September 1979.

Registrations: Required.

Administration: Appointed 5-member Rent Review Commission, (619) 323-8211.

Rent Formula: Rents may not be increased from their September 1979 levels by more than 75% of the total annual Consumer Price Indexes from September 1979.

Individual Adjustments: Landlords may apply to Rent Review Commission for further increases in the event of "extra-ordinary hardship."

Vacancy Decontrol: No.

Eviction Protection: Retaliation prohibited.

Other Features: Unlike the rent control ordinance of any other city, its provisions can be waived in writing, thus allowing landlords to coerce tenants into giving up protection under the ordinance. This is very bad, even though the ordinance allows a tenant victim of a coerced waiver to sue the landlord for $300.

200

SAN FRANCISCO

Exceptions: Units constructed since June 1979; Owner-occupied 4 units or less; Buildings over 50 years old if "substantially rehabilitated."

Registrations: No.

Administration: Appointed 5-member Rent Stabilization and Arbitration Board, 170 Fell Street, San Francisco, CA, (415) 621-RENT.

Rent Formula: Rent may not be increased more than from 4–7% in any 12 month period, except to pass on increased utility costs. The exact amount of the increase is calculated using a formula based on inflation.

Individual Adjustments: Landlord may apply to Board for higher than 7%* increase.

Vacancy Decontrol: Yes, if vacancy was "voluntary" or tenant was evicted for just cause.

Eviction Protection: San Francisco requires the landlord to have just cause to evict, after which the unit is no longer subject to rent control. This encourages landlords to find trivial "reasons" to evict in order to evade rent control. Retaliatory eviction prohibited.

Other Features: None.

SAN JOSE

Exceptions: New construction; Single-family houses; Duplexes.

Registrations: No.

Administration: Appointed 7-member Advisory Commission on Rents. Call Rent Unit, Room 200, 801 North Street, San Jose, CA, (408) 277-5431.

Rent Formula: Rents may not be increased more than 8% in any 12-month period, except that a landlord who has not raised the rent for 24 months is entitled to a 21% increase.

Individual Adjustments: **Warning:** Actually the landlord can raise the rent more than 8% without prior approval, and the tenant must petition the Commission to disallow the increase. After a hearing, a mediation officer decides if the proposed increase is "reasonable." He is required to deem it reasonable if he finds that it is no more than 5%, plus any increased costs of maintenance and operation and the amortized costs of any rehabilitation or capital improvements. If the increase exceeds this, whether it is reasonable depends on many factors (such as the "landlord's response to Proposition 13 savings," and the quality of maintenance). If the mediation officer decides the rent increase is unreasonable, he then tries to mediate the dispute, i.e., holds a couple of meetings where he tries to get the parties to come to some agreement. If either party is not satisfied with the results with the mediation officer, the case can be appealed to an arbitrator, who holds a hearing and finally decides the case. As to eviction and vacancy decontrol,

San Jose has the worst of both worlds—vacancy decontrol (no more rent control on a unit after tenant leaves) and no requirement that the landlord have just cause to evict. Hence, landlords are tempted to evict with 30-day notices in order to evade rent control. "Evasive" evictions, as well as retaliatory ones, can subject the landlord to criminal prosecution for a misdemeanor—but intent is hard to prove and prosecutions are few.

Vacancy Decontrol: Yes, if voluntary or for cause.
Eviction Protection: No.
Other Features: None.

SANTA MONICA

Exceptions: New construction; Owner-occupied 3 units or less. **Note:** These exemptions are not automatic—the landlords must apply for them.

Registrations: Required, or landlord can't raise rents and tenant can seek Board's permission to withhold rent.

Administration: Elected 5-member Rent Control Board, 1685 Main Street, Santa Monica, CA, (213) 394-9661.

Rent Formula: 4/10/79 at 4/78 levels, plus annual adjustments by Board after investigation and hearings. **Note:** Since April 1979, the following annual adjustments have been allowed: 1979, 7%; 1980, 6.5%; 1981, 5.5%; 1982, 5.5%; 1983, 4.5%. Landlord may apply for further increase due to "hardship" (does not include "negative cash flow" based on recent purchase), and tenant is notified of hearing.

Individual Adjustments: Landlord may apply for further increase due to "hardship" (does not include "negative cash flow" based on recent purchase), and tenant is notified of hearing. Tenant may seek rent reduction for poor maintenance.

Vacancy Decontrol: Board may remove category of housing with over 5% vacancy rate from controls; Board is required to conduct vacancy rate surveys. **Note:** All categories of housing have vacancy rates of about 1%, so that no categories have been removed from controls.

Eviction Protection: Just cause required for eviction. Retaliation prohibited.

Other Features: Establishes strict permit process for demolitions and condominium conversions. Interest on security depositions must be counted as income and/or returned to tenants.

202

Appendix 1

SAMPLE MODEL LEASE, MODEL RENTAL AGREEMENT AND CHECKLIST

Two printed 8½" x 14" copies of the Sample Model Lease and Model Rental Agreement forms and the checklist are available for $2.95 plus 6% tax from Nolo Press, 950 Parker Street, Berkeley, CA 94710. Ask for the Tenant Form Kit.

Lease

National Housing and Economic Development Law Project Standard Form Lease (California)

1. Parties

The parties to this agreement are _____

_____

_____

_____ , hereinafter called "Landlord,"

and _____

_____

_____

_____ , hereinafter called "Tenant."

If Landlord is the agent of the owner of said property, the owner's name and address is _____

_____

2. Property

Landlord hereby lets the following property to Tenant for the term of this agreement: (a) the property located at _____

_____

and (b) the following furniture and appliances on said property: _____

_____

_____

3. Term

The term of this agreement shall be for _____ , beginning on _____ and ending on

_____ .

4. Rent

The monthly rental for said property shall be $ _____ , due and payable on the first day of each month.

5. Utilities

Utilities shall be paid by the party indicated on the following chart:

	Landlord	Tenant
Electricity		
Gas		
Water		
Garbage collection		
Trash removal		
Other		

6. Use of Property

Tenant shall use the property only for residential purposes, except for incidental use in his trade or business (such as telephone solicitation of sales orders or arts and craft created for profit), so long as such incidental use does not violate local zoning laws or affect Landlord's ability to obtain fire or liability insurance.

7. Tenant's Duty to Maintain Premises

Tenant shall keep the dwelling unit in a clean and sanitary condition and shall otherwise comply with all state and local laws requiring tenants to maintain rented premises. If damage to the dwelling unit (other than normal wear and tear) is caused by acts or neglect of Tenant or others occupying the premises with his permission, Tenant may repair such damage at his own expense. Upon Tenant's failure to make such repairs, after reasonable notice by Landlord, Landlord may cause such repairs to be made and Tenant shall be liable to Landlord for any reasonable expense thereby incurred by Landlord.

8. Alterations

No substantial alteration, addition, or improvement shall be made by Tenant in or to the dwelling unit without the prior consent of Landlord in writing. Such consent shall not be unreasonably withheld, but may be conditioned upon tenant's agreeing to restore the dwelling unit to its prior condition upon moving out.

9. Noise

Tenant agrees not to allow on his premises any excessive noise or other activity which disturbs the peace and quiet of other tenants in the building. Landlord agrees to prevent other tenants and other persons in the building or common areas from similarly disturbing Tenant's peace and quiet.

10. Inspection by Landlord

Unless Tenant has moved out, Landlord or his agent may enter the dwelling unit only for the following purposes: to deal with an emergency (such as fire); to make necessary or agreed repairs, decorations, alterations or improvements; to supply necessary or agreed services; or to show the unit to prospective or actual purchasers, mortgagees, tenants, workmen, or contractors. Unless there is an emergency, Landlord must give at least 24 hours prior notice of his intent to enter and the date, time, and purpose of the intended entry. (In case of an emergency entry, Landlord shall, within 2 days thereafter, notify Tenant in writing of the date, time, and purpose of the entry.) Tenant shall have the right to refuse to allow any entry (except for an emergency) before 9 AM or after 5 PM. If Tenant objects to an intended entry between 9 AM and 5 PM, Landlord shall (where feasible) attempt to arrange a more convenient time for tenant. Landlord's entries shall not be so frequent as to seriously disturb Tenant's peaceful enjoyment of the premises and shall not be used to harass Tenant.

11. Security Deposit

a) Upon signing this agreement, Tenant shall deposit with Landlord the sum of $ _____ as a security deposit. This deposit (with any interest accrued under the subparagraph (c) of this paragraph) may be applied by Landlord toward reimbursement for any costs reasonably necessary to repair any damage to the premises caused by Tenant, to clean the premises (where Tenant has not left the premises as clean as he found them), or for due and unpaid rent.

b) Landlord shall inspect the premises within one week prior to Tenant's vacating the premises and, before Tenant vacates, shall give Tenant a written statement of needed repairs and the estimated cost thereof.

c) Within two weeks after Tenant vacates the premises, Landlord shall return to Tenant the security deposit together with interest of one-third of one per cent for each month Landlord held the deposit, less any deductions Landlord is entitled to make under subparagraph (a) of this paragraph. If Landlord makes any such deductions, he shall, within two weeks after Tenant vacates the premises, give Tenant a written itemized statement of such deductions and explanations thereof.

12. Landlord's Obligation to Repair and Maintain Premises

a) Landlord shall maintain the building and grounds appurtenant to the dwelling unit in a decent, safe, and sanitary condition, and shall comply with all state and local laws, regulations, and ordinances concerning the condition of dwelling units.

b) Landlord shall take reasonable measures to maintain security on the premises and the building and grounds appurtenant thereto to protect tenant and other occupants and guests of the premises from burglary, robbery, and other crimes. Tenant agrees to use reasonable care in utilizing such security measures.

c) As repairs are now needed to comply with this paragraph, Landlord specifically agrees to complete the following repairs by the following dates:

Repair	Date

d) If Landlord substantially fails to comply with any duty imposed by this paragraph, Tenant's duty to pay rent shall abate until such failure is remedied. This subparagraph shall apply to defects within Tenant's dwelling unit only if Tenant has notified Landlord or his agent of such defects and has given Landlord a reasonable time to make repairs. The remedy provided by this subparagraph shall not be exclusive of any other remedy provided by law to Tenant for Landlord's violation of this Agreement.

13. Subleasing

Tenant shall not assign this Agreement or sublet the dwelling unit without the written consent of Landlord. Such consent shall not be withheld without good reason relating to the prospective tenant's ability to comply with the provisions of this Agreement. This paragraph shall not prevent tenant from accomodating guests for reasonable periods.

14. Failure to Pay Rent

If Tenant is unable to pay rent when due, but on or before such due date he gives Landlord or his agent written notice that he is unable to pay said rent on time and the reasons therefore, Landlord shall attempt to work out with Tenant a procedure for paying such rent as soon as possible. If, after 10 days, Landlord and Tenant are unable to work out such a procedure, Landlord may serve a notice to pay rent or vacate within 3 days, as provided by California Code of Civil Procedure Section 1161.

15. Destruction of Premises

If the premises become partially or totally destroyed during the term of this Agreement, either party may thereupon terminate this Agreement upon reasonable notice.

16. Tenant's Termination for Good Cause

Upon 30 days written notice, for good cause, Tenant may terminate this Agreement and vacate the premises. Said notice shall state good cause for termination. Good cause shall include, but not be limited to, entry into active duty with U.S. military services, employment in another community, and loss of the main source of income used to pay the rent.

17. Termination

Upon termination of this Agreement, Tenant shall vacate the premises, remove all personal property belonging to him, and leave the premises as clean as he found them (normal wear and tear excepted), unless the property is located in an area covered by "just cause" for eviction regulations, in which case these rules control.

18. Lawsuits

If either party commences a lawsuit against the other to enforce any provision of this Agreement, the successful party shall be awarded court costs from the other. Landlord specifically waives any right to recover treble or other punitive damages pursuant to California Code of Civil Procedure Section 1174.

19. Notices

All notices and rent provided by this Agreement shall be in writing and shall be given to the other party as follows:
To the Tenant: at the premises.
To the Landlord: at _____

20. Holdovers

If tenant holds over upon termination of this Agreement and Landlord accepts Tenant's tender of the monthly rent provided by this Agreement, this Agreement shall continue to be binding on the parties as a month-to-month agreement. In this situation Tenant may terminate this Agreement upon 30 days' written notice to Landlord. Landlord may terminate or change the terms of this Agreement upon 60 days' written notice thereof to Tenant, unless the property is located in an area covered by "just cause" for eviction regulations, in which case these rules control.

WHEREFORE We, the undersigned, do hereby execute and agree to this Lease.

LANDLORDS: TENANTS:

_____   _____
(signature)   (signature)

_____   _____
(date of signature)   (date of signature)

_____   _____
(signature)   (signature)

_____   _____
(date of signature)   (date of signature)

Rental Agreement

National Housing and Economic Development Law Project Standard Form Rental Agreement (California)

1. Parties
The parties to this agreement are _____

_____

_____

_____ , hereinafter called "Landlord,"
and _____

_____

_____

_____ , hereinafter called "Tenant."
If Landlord is the agent of the owner of said property, the owner's name and address is _____

_____

2. Property
Landlord hereby lets the following property to Tenant for the term of this agreement: (a) the property located at _____

_____

and (b) the following furniture and appliances on said property: _____

_____

_____

3. Term
This Agreement shall run from month-to-month, beginning on _____

4. Rent
The monthly rental for said property shall be $_____ , due and payable on the first day of each month.

5. Utilities
Utilities shall be paid by the party indicated on the following chart:

	Landlord	Tenant
Electricity		
Gas		
Water		
Garbage collection		
Trash removal		
Other		

6. Use of Property
Tenant shall use the property only for residential purposes, except for incidental use in his trade or business (such as telephone solicitation of sales orders or arts and craft created for profit), so long as such incidental use does not violate local zoning laws or affect Landlord's ability to obtain fire or liability insurance.

7. Tenant's Duty to Maintain Premises
Tenant shall keep the dwelling unit in a clean and sanitary condition and shall otherwise comply with all state and local laws requiring tenants to maintain rented premises. If damage to the dwelling unit (other than normal wear and tear) is caused by acts or neglect of Tenant or others occupying the premises with his permission, Tenant may repair such damage at his own expense. Upon Tenant's failure to make such repairs, after reasonable notice by Landlord, Landlord may cause such repairs to be made and Tenant shall be liable to Landlord for any reasonable expense thereby incurred by Landlord.

8. Alterations
No substantial alteration, addition, or improvement shall be made by Tenant in or to the dwelling unit without the prior consent of Landlord in writing. Such consent shall not be unreasonably withheld, but may be conditioned upon tenant's agreeing to restore the dwelling unit to its prior condition upon moving out.

9. Noise
Tenant agrees not to allow on his premises any excessive noise or other activity which disturbs the peace and quiet of other tenants in the building. Landlord agrees to prevent other tenants and other persons in the building or common areas from similarly disturbing Tenant's peace and quiet.

10. Inspection by Landlord
Unless Tenant has moved out, Landlord or his agent may enter the dwelling unit only for the following purposes: to deal with an emergency (such as fire); to make necessary or agreed repairs, decorations, alterations or improvements; to supply necessary or agreed services; or to show the unit to prospective or actual purchasers, mortgagees, tenants, workmen, or contractors. Unless there is an emergency, Landlord must give at least 24 hours prior notice of his intent to enter and the date, time, and purpose of the intended entry. (In case of an emergency entry, Landlord shall, within 2 days thereafter, notify Tenant in writing of the date, time, and purpose of the entry.) Tenant shall have the right to refuse to allow any entry (except for an emergency) before 9 AM or after 5 PM. If Tenant objects to an intended entry between 9 AM and 5 PM, Landlord shall (where feasible) attempt to arrange a more convenient time for tenant. Landlord's entries shall not be so frequent as to seriously disturb Tenant's peaceful enjoyment of the premises and shall not be used to harass Tenant.

11. Security Deposit
a) Upon signing this agreement, Tenant shall deposit with Landlord the sum of $_____ as a security deposit. This deposit (with any interest accrued under the subparagraph (c) of this paragraph) may be applied by Landlord toward reimbursement for any costs reasonably necessary to repair any damage to the premises caused by Tenant, to clean the premises (where Tenant has not left the premises as clean as he found them), or for due and unpaid rent.

b) Landlord shall inspect the premises within one week prior to Tenant's vacating the premises and, before Tenant vacates, shall give Tenant a written statement of needed repairs and the estimated cost thereof.

c) Within two weeks after Tenant vacates the premises, Landlord shall return to Tenant the security deposit together with interest of one-third of one per cent for each month Landlord held the deposit, less any deductions Landlord is entitled to make under subparagraph (a) of this paragraph. If Landlord makes any such deductions, he shall, within two weeks after Tenant vacates the premises, give Tenant a written itemized statement of such deductions and explanations thereof.

12. Landlord's Obligation to Repair and Maintain Premises

a) Landlord shall maintain the building and grounds appurtenant to the dwelling unit in a decent, safe, and sanitary condition, and shall comply with all state and local laws, regulations, and ordinances concerning the condition of dwelling units.

b) Landlord shall take reasonable measures to maintain security on the premises and the building and grounds appurtenant thereto to protect tenant and other occupants and guests of the premises from burglary, robbery, and other crimes. Tenant agrees to use reasonable care in utilizing such security measures.

c) As repairs are now needed to comply with this paragraph, Landlord specifically agrees to complete the following repairs by the following dates:

Repair   *Date*

_____

_____

_____

_____

_____

d) If Landlord substantially fails to comply with any duty imposed by this paragraph, Tenant's duty to pay rent shall abate until such failure is remedied. This subparagraph shall apply to defects within Tenant's dwelling unit only if Tenant has notified Landlord or his agent of such defects and has given Landlord a reasonable time to make repairs. The remedy provided by this subparagraph shall not be exclusive of any other remedy provided by law to Tenant for Landlord's violation of this Agreement.

13. Subleasing

Tenant shall not assign this Agreement or sublet the dwelling unit without the written consent of Landlord. Such consent shall not be withheld without good reason relating to the prospective tenant's ability to comply with the provisions of this Agreement. This paragraph shall not prevent tenant from accomodating guests for reasonable periods.

14. Failure to Pay Rent

If Tenant is unable to pay rent when due, but on or before such due date he gives Landlord or his agent written notice that he is unable to pay said rent on time and the reasons therefore, Landlord shall attempt to work out with Tenant a procedure for paying such rent as soon as possible. If, after 10 days, Landlord and Tenant are unable to work out such a procedure, Landlord may serve a notice to pay rent or vacate within 3 days, as provided by California Code of Civil Procedure Section 1101.

15. Destruction of Premises

If the premises become partially or totally destroyed during the term of this Agreement, either party may thereupon terminate this Agreement upon reasonable notice.

16. Notice of Termination

Tenant may terminate this Agreement upon 30 days' written notice thereof to Landlord. Landlord may terminate or change the terms of this Agreement upon 60 days' written notice thereof to Tenant unless the property is located in an area covered by "just cause" for eviction regulations, in which case these rules control. No notice shall be valid, however, if the Landlord's dominant purpose in serving it is to retaliate against the Tenant because of Tenant's attempt to exercise or assert his rights under this Agreement or any law of the state of California, its governmental subdivisions, of the United States, or because of any other lawful act of Tenant. Any such notice shall contain a statement of the reasons for termination or change of terms, and if such statement be controverted, Landlord shall have the burden of proving its truth. This paragraph shall not affect Landlord's right to terminate for cause after expiration of a 3-day notice given pursuant to California Code of Civil Procedure Section 1161.

17. Termination

Upon termination of this Agreement, Tenant shall vacate the premises, remove all personal property belonging to him, and leave the premises as clean as he found them (normal wear and tear excepted).

18. Lawsuits

If either party commences a lawsuit against the other to enforce any provision of this Agreement, the successful party shall be awarded court costs from the other. Landlord specifically waives any right to recover treble or other punitive damages pursuant to California Code of Civil Procedure Section 1174.

19. Notices

All notices and rent provided by this Agreement shall be in writing and shall be given to the other party as follows:
To the Tenant: at the premises.
To the Landlord: at _____

WHEREFORE We, the undersigned, do hereby execute and agree to this Lease.

LANDLORDS: TENANTS:

_____   _____

(signature)   (signature)

_____   _____

(date of signature)   (date of signature)

_____   _____

(signature)   (signature)

_____   _____

(date of signature)   (date of signature)

CHECKLIST

The following is a summary of the condition of the premises at

_____, California,

on the dates indicated below.

	CONDITION ON ARRIVAL	CONDITION ON DEPARTURE
LIVING ROOM		
Floors & Floor Covering		
Drapes		
Walls & Ceilings		
Furniture (if any)		
Light Fixtures		
Windows, Screens & Doors		
Anything Else		
KITCHEN		
Floor Covering		
Stove & Refrigerator		
Windows, Screens & Doors		
Light Fixtures		
Sink & Plumbing		
Cupboards		
DINING ROOM		
Floor & Floor Covering		
Drapes		
Walls & Ceilings		
Furniture (if any)		
Light Fixtures		
Windows, Screens & Doors		
BATHROOM(S)		
Toilet(s)		
Sink(s)		
Shower(s)		
Floor, Walls & Ceiling		
Light Fixtures		
Windows, Screens j& Doors		
BEDROOMS		
Floors, Floor Covering		
Walls & Ceiling		
Furniture (if any)		
Windows, Screens & Doors		
Light Fixtures		
OTHER AREAS		
Floors & Floor Covering		
Windows, Screens & Doors		
Walls & Ceilings		
Furnace		
Air Conditioning (if any)		
Lawn, Ground Covering		
Patio, Terrace, Deck, etc.		
Other		

Checklist filled out on moving in on_____, 19____, and approved by

_____ and _____.
    Landlord   Tenant

Checklist filled out on moving out on_____, 19____, and approved by

_____ and _____.
    Landlord   Tenant

Appendix 2

THE FORM
ANSWER—UNLAWFUL DETAINER

Preprinted forms (Answer—Unlawful Detainer) are available free from any Municipal Court Clerk's (Civil Division) office. They may be (but don't have to be) used instead of the typed answer set forth in Chapter 11. You may use the preprinted form answer in all circumstances. It makes no difference that your landlord used a preprinted complaint or a typed one.

ATTORNEY OR PARTY WITHOUT ATTORNEY (NAME AND ADDRESS):	TELEPHONE:	FOR COURT USE ONLY
Raymond Gonzales 37 Arcadia St. Berkeley, CA	(415) 848-7200	

ATTORNEY FOR (NAME): In Pro Per

Insert name of court, judicial district or branch court, if any, and post office and street address:

Berkeley-Albany Municipal Court
2000 Center Street
Berkeley, CA

PLAINTIFF:

S & P Properties

DEFENDANT:

Raymond Gonzales

ANSWER—Unlawful Detainer	CASE NUMBER 42-791

1. This pleading including attachments and exhibits consists of the following number of pages: ___2___
2. Defendants *(name):*

   Raymond Gonzales

   answer the complaint as follows:
3. **Check ONLY ONE of the next two boxes:**

   a. ☐ Defendant generally denies each statement of the complaint. *(Do not check this box if the complaint demands more than $1,000.)*

   b. ☒ Defendant admits that all of the statements of the complaint are true EXCEPT:

   (1) Defendant claims the following statements of the complaint are false *(use paragraph numbers from the complaint or explain):*

   paragraphs 8, 11 & 13

   ☐ Continued on Attachment 3.b.(1).

   (2) Defendant has no information or belief that the following statements of the complaint are true, so defendant denies them *(use paragraph numbers from the complaint or explain):*

   paragraphs 7 & 12

   ☐ Continued on Attachment 3.b.(2).
4. **AFFIRMATIVE DEFENSES**

   a. ☒ *(nonpayment of rent only)* Plaintiff has breached the warranty to provide habitable premises. *(Briefly state the facts below in item 4.k.)*

   b. ☐ Plaintiff waived, changed, or canceled the notice to quit. *(Briefly state the facts below in item 4.k.)*

   c. ☒ Plaintiff served defendant with the notice to quit or filed the complaint to retaliate against defendant. *(Briefly state the facts below in item 4.k.)*

   d. ☐ Plaintiff has failed to perform his obligations under the rental agreement. *(Briefly state the facts below in item 4.k.)*

   e. ☐ By serving defendant with the notice to quit or filing the complaint, plaintiff is arbitrarily discriminating against the defendant in violation of the constitution or laws of the United States or California. *(Briefly state the facts below in item 4.k.)*

   f. ☒ Plaintiff's demand for possession violates the local rent control or eviction control ordinance of *(city or county, title of ordinance, and date of passage):*

   (Briefly state the facts showing violation of the ordinance in item 4.k.)

   (Continued)

Form Approved by the
Judicial Council of California
Effective January 1, 1982
Rule 982.1(95)

ANSWER—Unlawful Detainer

CCP 425.12

ANSWER—Unlawful Detainer

g. ☐ Plaintiff accepted rent from defendant to cover a period of time after the date stated in paragraph 8.b. of the complaint.

h. ☐ *(nonpayment of rent only)* On *(date):*   defendant offered the rent due but plaintiff would not accept it.

i. ☐ Defendant made needed repairs and properly deducted the cost from the rent, and plaintiff did not give proper credit.

j. ☐ Other affirmative defenses. *(Briefly state below in item 4.k.)*

k. FACTS SUPPORTING AFFIRMATIVE DEFENSES CHECKED ABOVE *(Identify each item separately.)*

   4A - On January 25, 198_ defendant asked plaintiff landlord to fix six leaks in the roof of the rental unit at 37 Arcadia St. This was not done. On February 1, 198_ defendant gave landlord a Notice of Intention to withhold rend because the premises were uninhabitable.

   4C - Plaintiffs attempt to evict defendant in this action is in retaliation for his decision to legally withhold rent until uninhabitable conditions were fixed.

   4F - The rent control ordinance of the City of Berkeley requires "just cause" for eviction. Plaintiff has claimed no such cause in his complaint.

   ☐ Continued on Attachment 4 k

5. OTHER STATEMENTS

   a. ☐ Defendant vacated the premises on *(date):*

   b. ☐ Defendant claims a credit for deposits of $_____

   c. ☐ The fair rental value of the premises in item 12 of the complaint is excessive *(explain):*

   d. ☐ Other *(specify):*

6. DEFENDANT REQUESTS

   a. that plaintiff take nothing requested in the complaint.

   b. costs incurred in this proceeding.

   c. ☒ reasonable attorney fees.

   d. ☐ other *(specify):*

Raymond Gonzales
....
(Type or print name)

_____
(Signature of defendant or attorney)

....
(Type or print name)

_____
(Signature of defendant or attorney)

(Each defendant for whom this answer is filed must be named in item 2 and must sign this answer unless represented by an attorney.)

VERIFICATION

(Use a different verification form if the verification is by an attorney or for a corporation or partnership.)

I am the defendant in this proceeding and have read this answer. I declare under penalty of perjury under the laws of the State of California that this answer is true and correct.

Date:

Raymond Gonzales
....
(Type or print name)

_____
(Signature of defendant)

ANSWER—UNLAWFUL DETAINER: How to Fill It Out

Top of the Form: This is self-explanatory. If you are representing yourself, put your name in both the box marked attorney and the one marked defendant. You will find the information for the "name of court" box and the "case number" box on the plaintiff's form which has been served on you.

Box 1: Fill in "2" unless you add attachments. If you do, use 8½ x 11" typing paper (numbered legal paper is not required), and clearly mark each attachment by labeling it with the paragraph on the printed form answer to which it refers (see sample attachment page below). Each attachment should be on one side of a separate sheet and should be stapled to the Answer—Unlawful Detainer Form.

Box 2: Fill in your name.

Box 3: Box 3 presents a fork in the road. You are required to take one direction or the other since the instructions say "Check ONLY ONE of the next two boxes". How do you know which direction to take?

First, does the complaint expressly ask for more than $1000 in damages? If it does not, check box a. If it does, check box b.

If you've checked box b, you have a little more work to do before going to box 4. Follow these directions and you should have no trouble:

Carefully read the Complaint paragraph by paragraph. As you do, take the following actions for each paragraph.

1. If you agree with everything in the paragraph, go on to the next one.

2. If you disagree with any statement in a paragraph, enter the paragraph number in the space on the Answer form after 3b(1). You may very well disagree with more than one paragraph. If so, enter the numbers of all such paragraphs. If you disagree with only part of a paragraph you should still list it here.

3. If you don't have enough information to agree or disagree with a statement in a paragraph, enter the paragraph number in the space on the Answer form labeled 3b(2).

NOTE: Make sure you do a careful job of reading each paragraph of the complaint. Any paragraph of the complaint which isn't listed after box 3b(1) or 3b(2) will be accepted as true. This means, unless you can absolutely agree with everything in each paragraph, the paragraph number should be entered on one of the two attachments, depending on whether you actually disagree with it or just can't say one way or the other.

Box 4: In earlier chapters, we described a number of possible defenses to evictions and referred to them as affirmative defenses. Just to refresh your memory, an affirmative defense is any defense which involves a set of facts different than those raised in the complaint. For example, suppose you are evicted because you didn't pay your rent. If your defense involves habitability questions, it is based on different facts than are found in the complaint and is therefore an affirmative defense. The purpose of raising affirmative defenses in an answer is to let the court and the other side know what your defense is all about. Of course, if your defense is simply based on a denial of the facts raised in the complaint, then you wouldn't need to raise any affirmative defenses. For example, if the landlord says that you didn't pay your rent, and you say you did, then all you have to do is deny the allegation that you didn't pay your rent. That's what box 3 was all about.

In box 4, and its subparts, you have an opportunity to raise a number of affirmative defenses, so long as they describe your particular circumstances. Not everyone has an affirmative defense, but many do.

This is the way box 4 works. For every affirmative defense listed on the form which describes your situation, you should check the appropriate box. Then, in Section 4(k), you are provided a little room to state the facts on which you base your affirmative defense. See the example on the following page. Although fewer words you use to describe your defense the better, sometimes the room provided will not be enough. If not, take a sheet of 8½ x 11" paper, label it "Affirmative Defenses, 4(k)" at the top, and then if you need more room, simply put the subsection involved (i.e., if you need more room to answer 4(d), then put

4(d) on the attachment you've prepared and put in your additional facts under the 4(d). Your attachment in this example would look like this:

Affirmative Defenses 4(k)

4(d): The reason I didn't water the lawn as required in my rental agreement was that the landlord never provided the hose (which he had agreed to do).

Attachment

Even though we discussed many of these affirmative defenses in earlier parts of the book, we'll give you some brief examples here as well and also refer you back to the earlier specific discussions. If for any reason you are having trouble with this form, or with the idea of affirmative defenses in general, you might wish to consult a lawyer about possible affirmative defenses in your particular case.

4(a) Breach of Warranty of Habitability (Chapter 7(B)(1))

If you are being evicted for non-payment of rent and the landlord has reason to know that there are deficiencies in your apartment affecting its **habitability,** you should check box 4(a) and put the details in 4(k) or the attachment. This is the defense you'll be using if you withheld rent after giving the landlord notice of the deficiencies. Also, however, you should use this defense if the landlord knew about the problems, even if **you** didn't send a formal notice.

SAMPLE: On December 25, 198 , I notified my landlord (the plaintiff in this action), that the heater in my apartment was broken and asked that it be fixed. This was not done. On January 1, 198 , instead of paying my rent, I notified the landlord that my apartment was uninhabitable and that I was withholding my rent until the heater was fixed.

4(b) Waiver of Notice (Chapter 10 and Chapter 11(D)(2))

Sometimes landlords get wishy washy after giving you a notice to quit and tell you to disregard it. Then, they change their mind again and try to evict you on the original notice. If this happens, you can defend on the ground that the original notice is no good anymore and cannot support an eviction. Remember: Unless you are given a valid notice to quit **and it remains valid,** the landlord has no right to bring eviction proceedings (unlawful detainer). If this fits your situation, check 4(b) and put the facts in 4(k) or on the attachment.

SAMPLE: My landlord served a notice to quit on me, but later told me that I could forget about it if I would pay $50.00 more a month rent. I did for a month, but then wasn't able to afford it. The next thing I knew I was served with an unlawful detainer complaint based on the original notice.

4(c) Retaliatory Eviction (Chapters 7 and 11)

In recent years, the courts have prevented evictions when they are brought to punish tenant activities involving:

1. Complaints to health or safety authorities;
2. The exercise of statutory rights such as the right to repair and deduct (see Chapter 7(B)(3));
3. The exercise of rights under rent control ordinances;
4. Organizing for rent strikes or other tenant protests; and
5. Any other exercise of a statutory or constitutional right.

The general idea is that a person should not be punished by the landlord just because they are invoking rights or remedies provided to them by the law and the constitution. This is a very common defense, and if you believe that your landlord is retaliating against you for one of the activities mentioned above, check box 4(c) and put the details in 4(k) or on the attachment.

SAMPLE: I believe the real reason I'm being evicted is that I complained to the fire department about the lack of fire extinguishers in the building and the landlord was cited for non-compliance with the local fire codes.

4(d) Breach of Rental Agreement Caused by Landlord's Breach of Agreement

Sometimes, a tenant will be forced to break a rental agreement because the landlord fails to live up to his or her end. For example, if the landlord evicts you for allowing garbage to accumulate, but the landlord failed to provide you garbage cans as required in the rental agreement, your defense is that your breach of the agreement was caused by the landlord's breach. If so, check box 4(d) and enter the details in 4(k) or on the attachment.

SAMPLE: The reason I didn't water the lawn as required in my rental agreement was that the landlord never provided the hose which was supposed to come with the premises.

4(e) Discriminatory Eviction (Chapter 5)

Landlords may not evict you for **any** characteristic unrelated to your ability to be a good tenant, and if you feel you are being ousted because of your race, religion, sexual preference, dress, children, or for any other arbitrary reason, check box 4(e) and put the details in 4(k) or on the attachment.

SAMPLE: I believe I'm being evicted because I recently joined the Hare Krishna group and the landlord doesn't like my appearance.

4(f) Rent Control Violations (Chapter 15)

Under most rent control ordinances, landlords may not evict you for exercising your rights under the ordinance (see retaliatory evictions). Also, in cities such as San Francisco, San Jose, Berkeley, Los Angeles and Santa Monica, you can be evicted only for certain reasons and by certain procedures. If you believe that your eviction does not comply with your local rent control ordinance, check box 4(f) and put the details in 4(k) or on the attachment.

SAMPLE: The landlord says the reason I'm being evicted is that he wants the apartment for a relative. I have reason to believe, however, that he just wants to get me out so he can raise the rent.

NOTE: In most of the rent control ordinances, the landlord must be acting in good faith and without ulterior motive. If you believe that these requirements are being violated, use this defense.

216

4(g) Acceptance of Rent (Chapter 11)

Once a landlord gives notice to quit, he or she cannot accept rent for the period after the notice becomes effective. For example, if you receive a 30 day notice to quit, any rent accepted for any part of the period after the 30 days are up cancels the notice and entitles you to remain. Tenants often are advised to send a rent check for the period after the notice has expired in the hopes that the landlord's greed will exceed his or her need. If this has happened in your case, check box 4(g).

4(h) Refusal to Accept Rent (Chapter 11)

A landlord cannot refuse to accept your rent and then evict you for failure to pay rent. This sometimes happens when a landlord gives you a 3 day notice to pay rent or quit and then refuses your offer of the rent within the 3 day period. If this has happened to you, simply check box 4(h) and fill in the date you tendered the rent.

NOTE: When you tender rent after a three day notice has been served on you, it's always a good idea to have a witness.

4(i) Refusal to Allow Credit for Repairs (Chapter 7)

Under Civil Code Sections 1941 and 1942, you are entitled to make repairs for certain items after you've given adequate notice (30 days, usually) to the landlord and the problem remains unfixed, and then deduct the amount from your next rent check. You can do this twice in any 12-month period, each time for an amount up to a month's rent. If the landlord refuses to credit you for your deduction and wants to evict you for non-payment of rent, check box 4(i).

4(j) Other Affirmative Defenses

Often, landlords will orally allow tenants to get behind on their rent, or make certain repairs to their premises in exchange for free rent, or make other agreements on which the tenant relies because of a good relationship with the landlord. Then, when a falling out occurs, the landlord will attempt an eviction on the basis of a particular tenant default and deny that any oral agreement was made. In such a case, you would have an affirmative defense based on the agreement and would check this box and place the details on 4(k) or on the attachment.

Box 5

5(a). If you have moved out by the time you get around to filing this answer, check this box. Remember, even though you've moved out, the landlord may be suing for money damages as well as to regain possession of the premises and it is important to file this answer to have your day in court on the damages, even though possession of the apartment is no longer at issue.

5(b). Add up all your deposits and list here. Generally speaking, all deposits must be returned if you have left the premises clean and undamaged (see Chapter 2(C)(1))

5(c). Although the landlord may not accept **rent** after the expiration of the notice to quit, the court will award the landlord the fair market rental value of the premises for the period of time between the expiration of the notice and the day the judgment is entered. If the premises had habitability problems (see Chapter 7(B)(1)), the premises may not be worth what the landlord was renting them for, and you should check this box and explain any problems which existed.

5(d). This box gives you a chance to say anything which the other boxes didn't.

Box 6

Here you need check only box 6(c), unless you feel you are entitled to some other remedy. You are entitled to reasonable attorney fees **if you win** and your rental agreement or lease provides that your landlord can recover them **if he or she wins.** (See Chapter 11(c).) Also, under most rent control ordinances, you are entitled to attorneys fees if you win and your landlord violated the rent control ordinance by evicting you.

Signature and Verification Lines

Sign as indicated. Verify your answer if the landlord's complaint was verified.

NOTE: See Chapter 11 for instruction about filing your papers, serving them on the plaintiff, and appearing in court.

Appendix 3

FORM INTERROGATORIES —
UNLAWFUL DETAINER

Interrogatories are questions submitted to one party in a lawsuit by the other side. The answers to these questions can often be used as evidence in court.* They can also be valuable to learn more about your landlord's case. Normally, they must be answered within 30 days after they are served.** If you fail to respond to interrogatories submitted to you, your landlord may go to court and seek an order compelling you to answer. If the judge decides that your failure to respond was not justified, he could order penalties against you. These could include striking (not letting you put on evidence about) defenses you claim, or even rendering a decision against you.***

Preprinted forms (Form Interrogatories — Unlawful Detainer) come designed to allow both landlord and tenant to ask each other questions about their respective cases. These are now available, complete with instructions, from the Court Clerk of all trial courts. They are also found in Appendix IVb of the California Rules of Court, which are available at any law library. Their use is strictly optional. This means that you may draft your own interrogatories, combine your questions with the preprinted ones, use only form questions, or submit no interrogatories at all. If you do ask your landlord questions by using interrogatories, you are allowed to ask only those questions which are relevant to your situation. Remember that your landlord has this right, too.

---

*For more detailed information about interrogatories and other techniques for discovering information, see CALIFORNIA CIVIL DISCOVERY PRACTICE, a Continuing Education for the Bar publication, available in law libraries.

**Where rent is at issue, a landlord may ask the court to hear the case in 20 days. This does not allow enough time to use the answers to your interrogatories. If this happens to you, you will need to ask the court for an "order shortening time." Either see a lawyer or prepare an order yourself using one of the California form books, such as CALIFORNIA FORMS ON PLEADING AND PRACTICE.

***Code of Civil Procedure, Section 2034.

FORM INTERROGATORIES REQUEST — UNLAWFUL DETAINER
Propounding Party:

Responding Party:
Set No.:

CASE NUMBER:

IN DETERMINING WHETHER TO USE THESE OR ANY INTERROGATORIES, YOU SHOULD BE AWARE THAT ABUSE CAN BE PUNISHED BY SANCTIONS, INCLUDING FINES AND ATTORNEY FEES (CODE CIV. PROC., § 128.5).

FAILURE TO ANSWER THESE INTERROGATORIES PROPERLY CAN BE PUNISHED BY SANCTIONS, INCLUDING CONTEMPT, FINES, ATTORNEY FEES AND LOSS OF YOUR CASE (SEE CODE CIV. PROC., §§ 128.5, 2034).

FOR DETAILS ON THE USE OF INTERROGATORIES AND INSTRUCTIONS FOR ANSWERING, SEE THE TEXT OF THE FORM INTERROGATORIES AND SECTION 2030 OF THE CODE OF CIVIL PROCEDURE AND THE CASES CONSTRUING IT.

Each numbered box below refers to a form interrogatory. Answer each question checked. *The text of the form interrogatories with definitions and instruction is in Division IVb of the Appendix to the California Rules of Court. Copies are available from the clerk of the court.*

70.0 General
- 70.1
- 70.2
- 70.3
- 70.4
- 70.5
- 70.6
- 70.7
- 70.8
- 70.9
- 70.10
- 70.11
- 70.12
- 70.13
- 70.14

71.0 Notice
- 71.1
- 71.2
- 71.3
- 71.4
- 71.5
- 71.6
- 71.7
- 71.8
- 71.9

72.0 Service
- 72.1
- 72.2
- 72.3

73.0 Malicious Holding Over
- 73.1
- 73.2
- 73.3

74.0 Rent Control and Eviction Control
- 74.1
- 74.2
- 74.3
- 74.4
- 74.5
- 74.6

75.0 Breach of Warranty to Provide Habitable Premises
- 75.1
- 75.2
- 75.3
- 75.4
- 75.5
- 75.6
- 75.7
- 75.8

76.0 Waiver, Change, Withdrawal, or Cancellation of Notice to Quit
- 76.1
- 76.2

77.0 Retaliation and Arbitrary Discrimination
- 77.1

78.0 Nonperformance of the Rental Agreement by Landlord
- 78.1
- 78.2

79.0 Offer of Rent by Defendant
- 79.1

80.0 Deduction from Rent for Necessary Repairs
- 80.1
- 80.2
- 80.3
- 80.4
- 80.5
- 80.6

81.0 Fair Market Rental Value
- 81.1
- 81.2
- 81.3

▶

. . . . *(TYPE OR PRINT NAME)* . . . .

(SIGNATURE OF PARTY OR ATTORNEY)

FORM INTERROGATORIES REQUEST — UNLAWFUL DETAINER

CCP 2036.5

If you use the Form Interrogatories — Unlawful Detainer, simply send the first-page request form (see sample at the end of this section) with the numbers of the questions you want answered checked. You do not have to send copies of the pages containing the questions. It's up to your landlord to get these from the Court Clerk.

The Interrogatories contain questions appropriate to ask for many common landlord-tenant situations. These include the following:

- YOUR LANDLORD SERVED YOU IMPROPERLY
  WITH A NOTICE TO QUIT
  (See Chapter 11, part D(2), for what to do if you think there was a technical error in serving you.)
- YOUR LANDLORD VIOLATED A LOCAL RENT CONTROL
  ORDINANCE BY RAISING YOUR RENT ILLEGALLY OR
  BY USING THE "PHONY RELATIVE CAPER" OR THE
  "PHONY REPAIR GAMBIT"
  (See Chapter 15 for a general discussion of local ordinances and exemptions, and part C of that chapter for how to fight back against these and other ploys landlords use to try to get around rent control ordinances.)
- YOU WERE JUSTIFIED IN WITHHOLDING RENT BECAUSE THE
  LANDLORD FAILED TO KEEP THE PLACE IN GOOD REPAIR
  (See Chapter 7 for a discussion of the landlord's responsibilities and a discussion of your rights and options if the place is uninhabitable.)
- THE LANDLORD MAY HAVE RETALIATED AGAINST YOU
  FOR EXERCISING YOUR RIGHTS
  (Retaliatory evictions are illegal. See Chapter 7 for approaches to dealing with them.)
- THE LANDLORD HAS DISCRIMINATED AGAINST YOU
  ON ILLEGAL GROUNDS
  (See Chapter 5 for a discussion of illegal bases of discrimination and what to do if a landlord discriminates illegally against you.)

Remember that the form interrogatories also contain questions your landlord may submit to you, designed to uncover information that will help him. For example, he can ask you questions if he claims:

- YOU FAILED TO PAY RENT YOU OWE
  (See Chapter 2, part G, for a discussion of your responsibilities as a tenant, and Chapter 7, part G, on when you are allowed to withhold rent.)

- YOU STAYED IN THE PLACE AFTER YOUR LEASE EXPIRED
  (See Chapter 9, part A, for what happens when the lease expires.)
- YOU WERE RESPONSIBLE FOR DAMAGE TO THE PROPERTY, NOISE OR ANOTHER NUISANCE WHICH COULD JUSTIFY YOUR EVICTION

or

- YOU VIOLATED ANY OF THE TERMS OF YOUR AGREEMENT OR LEASE

or

- YOU USED THE PLACE FOR AN ILLEGAL PURPOSE
  (See page 52 for a discussion of your responsibilities as a tenant, and Chapter 11, part D(3), on defending yourself when your landlord attempts to evict you.

NOTE: Because you are entitled to use interrogatories doesn't mean that you must or should do so. Generally, the purpose of interrogatories is to find out information you don't know about the facts of your landlord's case. If you feel you know exactly what your landlord's contentions will be and what evidence he will present in court, you probably don't need to ask any questions.

ABOUT THE AUTHORS

MYRON MOSKOVITZ is a native San Franciscan who received his law degree (with honors) from the University of California in Berkeley in 1964. Since then, he has served as a law clerk for the California Supreme Court, directed the Marysville office of California Rural Legal Assistance, and was the Chief Attorney of the National Housing Law Project in Berkeley. He has written many articles and a book on tenants' rights for lawyers, and he has won several important cases establishing new rights for tenants. He is now a law professor at Golden Gate University in San Francisco, and was appointed by Governor Brown to be Chairman of the State's Commission of Housing and Community Development.

RALPH WARNER lives in Berkeley, California. He is an attorney, but spends most of his time writing, lecturing and consulting with the aim of getting people to better understand their legal system. A graduate of Princeton University and Boalt Hall School of Law, Ralph is the former Deputy Director of the Contra Costa Legal Service Foundation. Earlier, he was legal assistant to Chief Judge Richard Chambers of the U.S. Court of Appeals. Warner is author of *The People's Guide to California Marriage and Divorce Law* (with Toni Ihara), and *Everybody's Guide to Small Claims Court.*

CHARLES E. SHERMAN has served as a Deputy District Attorney (Los Angeles and Contra Costa Counties), a Senior Attorney in Contra Costa Legal Services, and has been in private practice. He is best known as the author of *How To Do Your Own Divorce,* and founder of The Wave Project's Do Your Own Divorce Centers. He is also a co-author of *Protect Your Home With A Declaration Of Homestead.*

TONI LYNNE IHARA, the editor, is an attorney and graduate of the School of Law at the University of California at Davis. She has worked for the Legal Aid Society of Alameda County and is the co-author of *Protect Your Home With A Declaration Of Homestead* and *The People's Guide To California Marriage Law.*

nolo

self-help law books

How To Form Your Own California Corporation
All the forms, Bylaws, Articles, stock certificates and instructions necessary to file your small profit corporation in California.
Calif. Edition $21.95
Texas Edition $21.95
New York Edition $19.95

The Non-Profit Corporation Handbook
Includes all the forms, Bylaws, Articles & instructions you need to form a non-profit corporation in California.
Calif. Edition $21.95

Bankruptcy: Do It Yourself Step-by-step instructions and all the forms you need.
$14.95

Legal Care For Your Software Protect your software through the use of trade secret, trademark, copyright, patents, contracts and agreements. $24.95

The Partnership Book A basic primer for people who are starting a small business together. Sample agreements, buy-out clauses, limited partnerships. $17.95

Plan Your Estate: Wills, Probate Avoidance, Trusts & Taxes Making a will, alternatives to probate, limiting inheritance & estate taxes, living trusts, and more.
Calif. $15.95
Texas $14.95

Chapter 13: The Federal Plan to Repay Your Debts The alternative to straight bankruptcy. This book helps you develop a plan to pay your debts over a 3-year period. All forms & worksheets included. $12.95

Billpayers' Rights Bankruptcy, student loans, bill collectors & collection agencies, credit cards, car repossessions, child support, etc. Calif. only. $10.95

The California Professional Corporation Handbook All the forms & instructions to form a professional corporation. Calif. only. $24.95

Small Time Operator How to start & operate your own small business, keep books, pay taxes. $8.95

How to Do Your Own Divorce All the forms for an uncontested dissolution. Instructions included.
Calif. Edition $12.95
Texas Edition $12.95

California Marriage & Divorce Law
Community & separate property, debts, children, buying a house, etc. Sample marriage contracts, simple will, probate avoidance information. Calif. only. $14.95

After the Divorce: How to Modify Alimony, Child Support & Child Custody How to increase alimony or child support, decrease what you pay, change custody & visitation.
Calif. only. $14.95

The Living Together Kit Legal guide for unmarried couples. Sample will & living together contract. $14.95

Sourcebook For Older Americans Most comprehensive resource tool on income, rights & benefits of Americans over 55. Social security, Medicare, etc. $12.95

How to Adopt Your Stepchild How to prepare all forms & appear in court. Calif. only. $14.95

A Legal Guide For Lesbian/Gay Couples
Raising children, buying property, wills, job discrimination and more. $14.95

Start Up Money: How to Finance Your New Small Business How to write a business plan, obtain a loan package and find sources of small business finance. $17.95

How to Copyright Software Establish copyright, common mistakes and how to correct them, failure to register, problems with protection and the Computer Copyright Act.
$21.95

People's Law Review 50-state catalog of self-help law materials; articles & interviews. $8.95

Fight Your Ticket Preparing for court, arguing your case, cross-examining witnesses, etc. Calif. only. $12.95

Legal Research: How to Find and Understand the Law Comprehensive guide to doing your own legal research. $12.95

California Tenants' Handbook Everything tenants need to know to protect themselves.
California Edition $9.95
Texas Edition $6.95

Everybody's Guide to Small Claims Court Step-by-step guide to going to small claims court. $9.95

How to Change Your Name All the forms & instructions you need. Calif. only. $14.95

Homestead Your House All the forms and instructions you need. Calif. only $8.95

Marijuana: Your Legal Rights All the legal information users & growers need to guarantee their constitutional rights & protect their privacy. $9.95

Author Law Publishing contracts, copyright, royalties, libel & invasion of privacy. Includes index and glossary. $14.95

The Criminal Records Book Takes you through all the procedures available to get your records sealed, destroyed or changed. Forms & instructions. Calif. only. $12.95

Landlording Maintenance and repairs, getting good tenants, avoiding evictions, taxes, etc. $15.00

Your Family Records: How to Preserve Personal, Financial and Legal History Probate avoidance, joint ownership of property, genealogical research. For existing & future family generations. $12.95

Media Law: A Legal Handbook for the Working Journalist Censorship, libel & invasion of privacy. Newsroom searches, access to news sources, reporter's privilege and more. $14.95

How to Become A United States Citizen Explains the naturalization process from filing to the oath of allegiance. Text is in both English & Spanish. $9.95

■ ■ ■

29 Reasons Not to Go to Law School A humorous and irreverent look at the dubious pleasures of going to law school. $6.95

Murder On The Air An unconventional murder mystery set in Berkeley, Calif. $5.95

Order Form

TENANTS' HANDBOOK

"... this handbook offers much advice on how to deal with land-lords. Tips range from how to get your walls painted to how to handle yourself in small claims court."

— THE SATURDAY REVIEW

"The book is written in an easy to read style, with a minimum of complicated legalese ... This book explains how to limit rent in-creases, force the landlord to make repairs, get deposits back among other things."

— Susan Berman, S. F. EXAMINER

"... sharper than a serpent's tooth."

—Herb Caen, S. F. CHRONICLE

"I couldn't think of any questions left unanswered ... Buy one and share it around, maybe with your neighbors in the building."

—PHOENIX/student newspaper,
San Francisco State University

"The TENANTS' HANDBOOK is readable, accurate, turns you on to a whole new ball game. And when you consider its message the hand-book is insane.

—SUNDAZ/underground newspaper,
Santa Cruz